A Broader View of
Jesus Christ

John Van Auken

Living in the Light
Virginia Beach, Virginia USA

Initial Edition
Copyright © 2004 John Van Auken
Expanded Edition
Copyright © 2015 John Van Auken

An initial version was titled
Christ: The Story and the Passion

JohnVanAuken.com
JohnVanAuken.newsletter@gmail.com

Living in the Light
P.O. Box 4942
Virginia Beach VA 23454 USA

Available from
Amazon.com, CreateSpace.com,
and other retail outlets

"'Your father Abraham rejoiced to see my day; and he saw it, and was glad.' The Jews therefore said unto him, 'Thou art not yet fifty years old, and hast thou seen Abraham?' Jesus said unto them, 'Verily, I say unto you, Before Abraham was born, I am.'" (John 8:56-58)

CONTENTS

A Note About Bible Quotes
A Note About Sources

1 Those People, Those Times p. 8
The First Jewish Nation
Israel and Judah
Assyrian Invasion
Babylonian Destruction of the Nation and the Temple
Persian Salvation and Rebuilding the Temple
The Great Diaspora
The Greek Gift
Weight of Roman Governance
Crushing Collapse and Dispersion
Jerusalem after Rome

2 The Incarnation of Jesus p. 31
Intro: Genealogy, Birth, and Flight to Egypt
Childhood Years in Nazareth
Journeys with the Magi
The Forerunner - John the Baptist
Jesus' Ministry
The Passion
Resurrection
The Ascension and the Holy Spirit

3 Forerunners and Early Christians p. 81
Essenes (Dead Sea Scrolls)
Gnostics (Nag Hammadi Scrolls)

4 The Journey of Christianity p. 107
Early Christian Movement
The Empire and the Church
The Inquisition
The Protestant Reformation
The Catholic Reformation
Ecumenical Efforts

5 The Mystical, Metaphysical Messiah-Christ p. 137
In the Image of God
Children of God
Christ Consciousness
Fruits of the Spirit

6 The Life of Saint Issa p. 157

7 About Islam p. 185

A Note about Bible Quotes

Throughout this book the World English Bible (WEB) translation is used or, on occasion, the 1901 American Standard Version (ASV). These are used because their translations are copyright free. When using the American Standard Version, I have modernized the language, sentence structure, and syntax of this classic translation to better approximate the way we read and speak today. The World English Bible is in modern English.

A Note about Sources

Most of the sources for information in this book are common historical records, but there are two sources that are from the "Akashic Records." The *Akasha* is an ancient concept that has its origin in the oldest body of religious literature yet discovered in the world, the *Rig Veda*, circa 1300 BC, a collection of more than a thousand hymns written in an archaic form of Sanskrit, one of the oldest languages on Earth. The central myth in the *Rig Veda* is the myth of creation, told in several different ways. *Akasha* refers to the essence of life and the records of its activity since, during, and following the creation. It is a record that is recorded in the "ethers," not in stone or on parchment. It has been referred to as "The Book of Life" or "The Book of Remembrance." It may also be thought of as a collective mind upon which all the activities and thoughts of every individual mind make an impression, an impression that can be known or "read" at a later time. The natural inclination to question such sources is understandable. Nevertheless, their content is included to give as full a picture of human knowledge on these topics as possible, leaving the reader to discern the value of this information.

The two akashic sources are *The Aquarian Gospel of Jesus Christ* by Levi, who was Levi H. Dowling. He was born on May 18, 1844, in Belleville, Ohio. His father was a pioneer preacher among the Disciples of Christ. Levi was always a student of the deeper things of life. While still a boy, he had a vision in which he was told that he was to "build a white city." This vision was repeated three times in his life. At the age of thirteen, in his first public debate, he took the negative side against a Presbyterian Elder on "The Everlasting Punishment of the Wicked." He began preaching at the age of sixteen, and at the age of eighteen was pastor of a small church. He entered the United States Army at the age of twenty as a Chaplain and served in this capacity until the end of the Civil War. From 1866 to 1867 he was a student at Northwestern Christian University in Indianapolis, Indiana. The next year he began publishing Sunday school literature, issuing Sunday school lesson papers, songbooks, and a children's Sunday school paper. Much of his time was devoted to the cause of Prohibition. He was a graduate of two medical colleges and practiced medicine for a number of years. He finally retired from the medical profession to resume literary work. The building of the "white city" was believed to be his manuscript, *The Aquarian Gospel of Jesus the Christ*. This book was transcribed between the early morning hours. He rose around 2 a.m. and, in a prayerful state, wrote until about 4 or sometimes 6 a.m. He received the information as the ancient prophets did. He sought to record the events in Jesus' life from childhood to his ministry, which are left out of the Gospels we have today. Levi died on August 13, 1911.

The second akashic source is the material from the American mystic Edgar Cayce (pronounced, KAY-see). These discourses were called "readings," because Cayce felt that he was reading the Book of Life or the Akashic Record. He was born on a farm near Hopkinsville, Kentucky, on March 18, 1877. As a child, he displayed unusual powers of perception. At the age of six, he told his parents that he could see "visions," sometimes of relatives who had recently died, sometimes of angels. He could also sleep with his head on his schoolbooks and awake with a photographic recall of their contents. Cayce would go into a hypnotic state to diagnose and prescribe healing for others, with so much success that doctors around Hopkinsville and Bowling Green took advantage of Cayce's unique talent to diagnose their patients. They soon discovered that all Cayce needed was the name and address of a patient to "tune in" telepathically to that individual's mind and body. The patient didn't have to be near Cayce, he could tune-in to them wherever they were. Eventually, Edgar Cayce, following advice from his own readings, moved to Virginia Beach, Virginia, and set up a hospital where he continued to conduct his "readings" for the health of others. But he also began a new line of readings called "Life Readings." From 1925 through 1944, he conducted some 2,500 of these Life Readings. Included in these were remarkable readings about Jesus Christ. When Cayce died on January 3, 1945, he left 14,256 documented stenographic records of the readings he had given for more than 6,000 different people over a period of forty-three years. I have modernized the language, sentence structure, and syntax of his discourses to better approximate the way we read and speak the language today. Since his discourses are indexed and available on CD-ROM for further study, I've included the reference numbers. The Edgar Cayce material is copyrighted by the Edgar Cayce Foundation and may not be used without permission.

    The reader can judge for him- or herself whether these two akaskic sources are valuable to the fuller understanding of a broader story of Jesus Christ and many other souls that were involved.

A BROADER VIEW

CHAPTER ONE
THOSE PEOPLE, THOSE TIMES

For the Western religious world, the story begins in Eden. Eden literally means "delight." The Bible identifies it as an ancient land at the confluence of the Tigris and Euphrates Rivers, and two other rivers that have disappeared: the Pishon and Gihon rivers. The Pishon is now considered to have been the long dried-up Kuwait River recently discovered by satellite imagery. The Tigris and Euphrates converge in the ancient land of Mesopotamia (Greek for "between the rivers"), which is today Iraq. From Eden, the people spread outward. Cain and his people headed east to the land of Nod, which is today Afghanistan. Legend has it that Cain's body was buried at the foot of a hill south of the city of Kabul. Eventually, the patriarch Abraham (circa 1996-1801 BC) and his people journeyed from Ur of the Chaldeans (its ruins are located between Baghdad and the head of the Persian Gulf, the site is now known today as Tall al Muqayyar, Iraq) to the land of Canaan (the land west of the Jordan River). Both Jews and Arabs trace their lineage directly to Abraham. Arab Muslims trace their lineage to Abraham's first-born son Ishmael, and the Ishmaelites. The Jews trace their line through Abraham's second son Isaac, Isaac's son Jacob, and Jacob's twelve sons, who are the fathers of the twelve tribes of the Israelites. However, many believe that the actual nation of the Israelites began with David and the city of Jerusalem. And Christians also associate Jesus' spiritual origins with David as well (Jesus being identified as "the root and the offspring of David," Revelation 22:16). Let's begin the story in Jerusalem with King David.

THE FIRST JEWISH NATION

Around 1000 BC, David, an outlaw in Saul's kingdom and a refugee among the Philistines, eventually was anointed King of Judah. After seven difficult years of struggle, he gained control over the northern tribes and became king of all the Israelites. He captured the city of Jebus, which Joshua had not been able to do, and changed its name to Jerusalem (literally meaning, "founded peaceful," as in "city of peace"). It became the City of David, the Holy City. Here he established the capital of his new national monarchy. He brought the Ark of the Covenant from an obscure retreat into the new Israelite city. David planned to erect a temple to house the Ark, but in those times the portability of the Ark was held as a divinely established feature, and the people could not let go of that requirement. By the time his son Solomon became king (961 BC), the people's feelings about portability had faded, and thus the great Temple was built of stone on the Temple Mount in the heart of the city. Records indicate that the Temple likely had an attached library and school. Eventually, Israelites dominated all of Palestine. These were grand times for the Jews. The Israelite court welcomed many foreign delegates – Cretans, Hittites, Philistines, and even Ishmaelites (ancestors of modern Arabs, also children of Abraham and the handmaid Hagar). Judging from Solomon's many diplomatic marriages to foreign princesses, there was an active attempt to get along with the neighboring nations, even though many were considered pagan. Solomon also allowed his princesses and their fathers to build pagan shrines to their gods in the Holy City, even on the Mount of Olives.

ISRAEL AND JUDAH

After Solomon's death (922 BC), growing religious opposition, combined with anger over the monarchy's forced labor for state projects, led to the nation dividing into two major groups. The northern tribes, headed by the tribe of Joseph, split away from the southern tribes, led by the tribe of Judah. The northern region became known as Israel (the name given by an angel to Jacob, the father of Joseph, meaning "he who strives with God"), while the southern region was called Judah, later Judea. Jerusalem remained the capital of Judah, while Samaria (no connection with Sumeria) became the capital of Israel.

THE ASSYRIAN INVASION

In 721 BC, Samaria fell to the Assyrians, as did Gilead and Galilee. Isaiah prophesied that Assyria was "the rod of God's wrath" against Israel. Judah was surrounded as well, and Jerusalem would have fallen, except that an epidemic decimated the Assyrian forces (2 Kings 19:35). But there wasn't much joy in Jerusalem, because the prophet Micah, a contemporary of Isaiah's and also a Judahite prophet, shocked his listeners by prophesying the coming loss of Jerusalem and the Temple mount! In the 600s BC, the prophets Jeremiah and Ezekiel continued the visions of doom for Israel and Judah, including the loss of the great Temple that Solomon had built.

As the Assyrian monarchy collapsed (circa 612 BC), the Babylonian monarchy arose and threatened the whole of the divided Jewish nation.

BABYLON

In 597 BC, Babylon forced Israel into submission, and in 586 BC all the prophecies came true, when King Nebuchadnezzar and the armies of Babylon invaded Judah, burnt the great Temple, and deported the population of Judah to Babylon. Those who managed to get away were scattered throughout the surrounding lands. All seemed lost.

Some believe that the Ark of the Covenant was stealthily sailed down the Nile and hidden in Aswan, Egypt, on Elephantine Island for a time, later to be transported into Ethiopia. Others believe that the Babylonians destroyed it. One fascinating insight on this matter comes from the reading of the Akashic records by Edgar Cayce: "Why – why was so little thought expressed as to where was the Ark of the Covenant, that was to remain ever in the Holy of Holies? It had *not* been destroyed, and was not destroyed, nor removed, until the Prince of Peace came, wherein there was the declaration that 'neither in this city nor in this mountain, but in the hearts of men' will there be the meeting in the Holy of Holies." (Cayce, 1000-14) Cayce is referring to Jesus' comments to the women at the well, recorded in the Gospel of John, 4:20-24: "Believe me, the hour comes, when neither in this mountain, nor in Jerusalem, will you worship the Father ... The hour comes, and now is, when the true worshippers will worship the Father in spirit and truth, for the Father seeks such to be his worshippers. God is spirit, and those who worship him must worship in spirit and truth." Cayce's reading of the Akashic Record indicates that the Ark was destroyed *after* Jesus, probably by the Roman General Titus, who destroyed the rebuilt Temple in 70 AD, presumably with the Ark inside of it. However, Cayce's words could mean that the Ark no longer works as it once did. If it does still work, and is hidden in Ethiopia, the Israelis would surely have brought it back to Jerusalem by now. Here's another Cayce reading on this shift of the Ark from an external device for communicating with God to an internal one within each of us: "Do stay close to the Ark of the Covenant which is *within* you; knowing the Father, the Son, the Holy Ghost must move within and through you if you would bring yourself closer to the fullness of your purposes in the earth." (Cayce, 5177-1)

Israel, Judah, and the great Holy City were first destroyed during the Babylonian invasion. Now the nation of the Israelites was gone and their great Temple destroyed.

Amazingly, Judaism survived in exile; even those in captivity in Babylon (mostly the Jews of Judah) managed to maintain their practices without a sanctuary or altar. This forced them to develop private prayer activity, small group ceremonies and discussions (the forerunners of the synagogue), and a literary cache to keep the history and teachings of the sacred documents alive. Also, they lost their way of life as landowners, forcing them to become professionals, traders, and bankers. Numerous cuneiform tablets in Babylon indicate that they became very good at these jobs. Surprisingly, the spirit of the exiles was so high that many non-Jews attached themselves to the groups because they believed these people would rise again, and they wanted to share in their future glory.

PERSIAN SALVATION AND REBUILDING THE TEMPLE

The prophecy had always been that 70 years were given to the punishment of Israel and Judah under the heel of Babylon. In 550 BC, Persia rose in power and challenged Babylon's control in the region. Cyrus the Great and Cyrus II were seen by many as the great instrument of God's salvation. They allowed the Jews in Persia and Babylon to return to Jerusalem, and the Persians even helped them establish homes and rebuild their temple by sending back with them the sacred vessels that had been taken from the first temple and a huge sum of money with which to buy building materials.

Over time, some 40,000 Jews made their way back to Jerusalem. Many Jews did not return to Jerusalem but stayed in Babylon and Persia. Those who did return began to rebuild the Temple (538-516 BC). But they became disillusioned by their struggles with the people who had established themselves in the region during the exile, the Samaritans. Samaritans were a Jewish mixture of native northern Israelites and Gentile deportees from Assyria. Also at this time, Hebrew had been replaced by Aramaic as the common language.

But Jews were still vulnerable to whims of the powers that ruled, and it was a woman was God's next instrument of salvation for the Jews; and that woman was Esther. There are only two books in the Bible titled after women: the Book of Ruth and the Book of Esther. However, only orthodox Protestants and Catholics include all verses of the Book of Esther. Current Protestant Bibles eliminate 103 verses from their editions.

Esther is a beautiful young Jewess who lived in Persia some 100 years after the Babylonians captured the people of Judah, including the prophet Daniel. Esther was an orphan and under the care of her older cousin Mordecai, an official in the Persian government of Susa, the capital of Persia. When the king of Persia, Xerxes I (519-465 BC), threw a lavish party to find a queen, Mordcai brought his young charge to the ball. She was the most beautiful woman there, and Xerxes chose her to be his queen. Later, Mordecai learned of a plot to kill the king. Rather than go directly to the king, he told Esther of the plot, and she warned her husband, also giving credit to Mordecai. The plot was thwarted. But all was not safe, for the king's highest official was Haman, who deeply hated the Jews, especially Mordecai who had once refused to bow to Haman. Haman convinced Xerxes that the Jews were evil and should all be killed. Xerxes approved Haman's plan to draw lots and kill each Jew chosen by lot. Mordecai said to Esther, "Do not think that because you are in the king's house that you alone of all the Jews will be spared. If you remain silent, relief and deliverance of the Jews will arise from other place, but you and your father's family will perish. And who knows that you have may come to your high royal position for this very moment!" (Esther 4:13-14)

Esther then urged all the Jews to fast and pray for deliverance. And then risking her own life, she approached Xerxes with a plan of her own. She invited Xerxes and Haman to a banquet where she revealed her Jewish heritage. Xerxes, who had come to love and appreciate Esther and her ways, broke out in a rage against Haman's accusations that Jews were evil, and ordered Haman impaled on the very same stake he had made to impale Mordecai. Then Xerxes promoted Mordecai to Haman's high office. Xerxes then granted his protection to all the Jews in the land.

For all the benefits that Persian rule brought to the Jews, it still represented subservience to an empire, which didn't sit well with a people who believed that only God ruled and directed them. In 444 BC, the Persian King Artaxerxes granted a charter to Ezra, empowering him to enforce the Torah as the imperial law for the Jews of the province "beyond the river" (that river being the Jordan), in which the district of Judah (now a small area) was located. The Torah (also called the Pentateuch, literally, the "five scrolls": Genesis, Exodus, Leviticus, Numbers, and Deuteronomy) is the first of three parts of Jewish law.

Despite all of the changes and challenges placed upon the restored Judahite community, they maintained a spirit of repentance and a desire to win back God's favor by adherence to the Mosaic Law. Unfortunately, this caused Judahite Jews to be suspicious of all strangers, which resulted in a lasting conflict with the Samaritans, even though they were fellow Jews. Judahites believed that they could become contaminated by passing through Samaritan territory. Judahites who traveled between Judea and Galilee would cross over the Jordan River to avoid Samaria, and then cross back over the river once they reached their destination. Samaritans claimed to have an older copy of the Torah than the Judahites and boasted that they observed the precepts better. The Judahites rejected the Samaritan copy of the law and publicly announced that Samaritans were not of any Jewish birth (John 4:12). The Samaritans asked permission to take part in the rebuilding of the great Temple, the Temple of the same God that both groups worshipped. The Judahites rejected them on ethno-religious grounds. Over the next several centuries, the divide between these two Jewish groups became a chasm. Samaritan Jews were publicly condemned in Judahite synagogues. Samaritans could not serve as witnesses in Judahite courts. Judahites believed that Samaritans had no place in the heavenly afterlife. Given this history, one can see how scandalous were Jesus' interactions with the Samaritan woman at the well and how his parable of the Good Samaritan stung deeply.

Throughout all of this there was a constant tension between messianic expectations and the grim reality of the restoration that lay before them. The inability to restore the glory of the past caused many to believe that God continued to be displeased with the Jews, the so-called "Chosen People." As time passed and messianic hopes remained unfulfilled, there grew a sense that a permanent suspension of normal relations with God had taken hold, and prophecy died out. Malachi was the last prophet (397 BC). He left this one last vestige of hope: "Behold, I will send you Elijah the prophet before the great and terrible day when the Lord comes." (Malachi 4:5) Many watched for Elijah's return, hoping that it signaled the return to better days.

THE GREAT DIASPORA

As a result of the dispersion and deportation, large, dynamic Jewish communities developed beyond Jerusalem and Palestine. This new world of Jews was called the

Diaspora, from a Greek word that means "dispersion." The dispersed communities were in Syria, Asia Minor (Turkey), Babylon (Iraq), Persia, and Egypt. Each of these communities had at least 1,000,000 Jewish inhabitants! The large community in Antioch – which, according to the historian Flavius Josephus, had been given all the rights of citizenship by the Seleucid king, Nicator – attracted a large number of converts to Judaism (around 250 BC). It was in Antioch that the apocryphal book of Tobit was composed around 100 BC. This book encouraged Diaspora Jews to hold fast to their faith. The largest and most important community of Diaspora Jews was in Egypt. There are several papyruses that indicate a Jewish military colony had a synagogue on Elephantine Island in Upper Egypt (Aswan) as early as the 500s BC.

THE GREEK GIFT

Finally, the Persian Empire fell to the Greeks, led by Alexander the Great (334 BC). After Alexander's death in 323 BC, his generals divided the kingdom among themselves. Seleucus, Alexander's youngest and strongest general, ruled the eastern provinces: Afghanistan, Iran, Iraq, Syria, and Lebanon, together with parts of Turkey, Armenia, Turkmenistan, Uzbekistan, and Tajikistan. Ptolemy ruled Egypt, but his authority included the area of Palestine, which was conquered in 332 BC, making it part of the Hellenistic kingdom. But the Greeks, like the Persians, were sensitive to the Jews and their culture. Greek writers recorded the Jews to be brave, self-disciplined, and philosophical. Alexander the Great assigned a quarter of his personal city, Alexandria, to the Egyptian Jews. In the 200s BC, the Torah was translated into Greek (known as the Septuagint). Ptolemaic rule allowed the Jews considerable cultural and religious freedom.

However, this merging was dangerous. In some ways it was like the Trojan Horse, beautiful on the outside but dangerous on the inside. It is believed by most scholars that the Hellenistic influence had become so pervasive among the Jews of Judea that, if the cultural merge had been allowed to go any further, true Jewish culture and religion would have been completely lost. However, Essene Jews, according to historian Josephus, sought refuge from all of these cultural and political machinations and went into complete isolation from the national life of the rest of the Jews. Essene goals were toward an ascetic life, based on living this life in preparation for the next, more important life. But in 198 BC, the Syrian Seleucid dynasty (descendants of Alexander's general, Seleucus) took over the Palestinian regions and granted the Jews a charter to govern themselves according to the Torah and their cultural traditions. Surprisingly, Hellenized Jews did not take hold of this new opportunity. They had come to enjoy and admire Greek ways. They gained control of the priesthood itself, appointing the High Priest. Their first High Priest, Jason (175-172 BC), established Jerusalem as a Greek city, Antioch-at-Jerusalem, with Greek educational institutions! The Seleucid Syrians, inclined to Greek culture and customs, encouraged such feelings. But the old priest, Mattathias, and his five sons – known as the Maccabees – rebelled against this continued Greek culturalization process.

Some believe that the Essene Dead Sea Scroll found at Qumran, entitled *War of the Sons of the Light Against the Sons of Darkness*, mirrors the fierce struggle between these two Jewish persuasions. The Hellenistic Jews (mostly Sadducees) had turned the Temple into a virtual bank, where the Temple wealth was kept and where private individuals deposited money. Opposition to this came from the scribes, who were interpreters and instructors of the Torah. A special group of scribes known as Hasidim or

"Pietists" became the forerunners of the Pharisees. These forerunners of the Pharisees joined in the struggle against the Hellenistic influences. Pharisees were middle-class Jews who interpreted the Torah to fit the times they lived in and accepted the Oral Law to be as important as the Written Law. On the other hand, the Sadducees, who were deeply influenced by Hellenization, were wealthy, conservative Jews who accepted the Torah literally and, like the Samaritans, refused to accept the Oral Law.

In 164 BC, the Maccabees successfully overcame the Seleucid Syrian influence, and the Temple was purified; this is the origin of the Jewish festival of Hanukkah (John 10:22). Grudgingly, the Seleucid Syrians recognized the autonomy of the Jews and the Jewish state. But it wasn't long before the Romans rose to power and threatened the area again. The Pharisees took a position of not opposing the Romans, but attempting to coexist with them. The Jewish population in Palestine at this time has been estimated to have been between one and five million. The Jewish population in the Diaspora is estimated to have been around five million, with the general opinion being that about ten percent of the Mediterranean world at the beginning of the Christian era was Jewish.

As Greek power waned, the Roman Empire rose in its place.

THE WEIGHT OF ROMAN GOVERNANCE

In 63 BC, the Roman general Pompey conquered Palestine and Jerusalem. At the time of Jesus' birth, greater Judea was ruled by the pro-Roman leader, Herod the Great (73 BC to 4 AD). None other than Mark Antony had appointed Herod ruler of the Jewish nation. Initially, Herod sought to rebuild the Jewish nation; bringing the high priest Hyrcanus back from Babylon. Together Herod and Hyrcanus oversaw an extensive building project, which included new walls around Jerusalem and a citadel that

A Broader View

guarded the remnants of great Temple. Herod named the citadel *Antonia* in honor of his patron Mark Antony. But, as history reveals, Mark Antony had divided the Roman Empire in two, Antony ruling the Eastern Empire from Egypt with his lover, Cleopatra, while Octavian and the Senate ruled the Western Empire from Rome. Unfortunately, Herod was backed by the wrong Roman, because in 31 BC Mark Antony and Cleopatra were defeated. In a mad panic, Herod the Great had Hyrcanus executed to ensure that no one else could claim his throne. Then he sailed to the island of Rhodes, where he met Octavian. In a brilliant speech, Herod boasted of his loyalty to Mark Antony and promised the same loyalty to the new master of the Roman Empire. Octavian was impressed by Herod's audacity, and declared Herod king of the Jewish nation, even adding the coast of Judea and Samaria to his realm. Herod returned to Judea and built a new market, an amphitheater, a theater, a new building where the Sanhedrin (the ruling council of the Jews) could convene, a new royal palace, and in 20 BC he started to rebuild the great Jewish Temple. He also built new buildings in Jericho and Samaria, and a new port in Caesarea in honor of the emperor. This magnificent and opulent city, which was dedicated in 9 BC, was built to rival Alexandria in the land trade with Arabia, from which spices, perfume, and incense were imported. It was not an oriental town like Jerusalem; it was laid out as a Greek city would be, with a market, an aqueduct, government offices, baths, villas, a circus, and pagan temples. The most important of these was a temple where the emperor himself was the object of worship. This upset many of the Jewish people.

In addition to his building accomplishments, Herod was developing a mighty army. He had already defeated the Arabs from Petra, Jordan, in 31 BC and repeated this in 9 BC. In 23 BC, Iturea and the Golan Heights were added to Herod's realms, and in 20 BC several other districts. The

Romans became increasingly uncomfortable with his independent behavior. The orthodox Jews came to hate the king because he was bringing Roman and Greek influences into their culture. The Sadducees hated him because he had terminated the rule of the old royal house, to which many of them were related and their influence in the Sanhedrin was eliminated. The Pharisees despised Herod because he increasingly ignored Jewish traditions and law, preferring the Greco-Roman ways. All of Herod's subjects resented his excessive taxation. According to Josephus, there were two taxes, at the annual rates equivalent to 10.7 percent and 8.6 percent, which were extremely high for any pre-industrial society (*Jewish Antiquities*, 14.202-206). Herod often had to resort to violence, employing mercenaries and secret police to enforce his will.

It was becoming increasingly clear that Herod was not a Jewish but a Roman king. He had become the ruler of the Jews with Roman help, and he boasted that he was *philokaisar*, "the emperor's friend." He erected on top of the gate of the new Temple a golden eagle, a symbol of Roman power in the heart of the holy city. All pious believers resented this. Worse, Emperor Augustus (Octavian's new name) ordered and paid the priests of the Temple to do sacrifices twice a day, on behalf of the Roman Emperor, the senate, and the Roman people. The Jewish populace started to believe rumors that their ruler had violated Jewish tombs, even stealing golden objects from the tomb of David!

But three events sealed Herod's fall from power: First, the monastery at Qumran, the home of the Essenes, was deliberately destroyed by fire in 8 BC. Many felt that Herod was responsible. In retaliation, when the king fell ill, two popular teachers, Judas and Matthias, incited their pupils to remove the golden eagle from the entrance of the

Temple. For this act, seen by many as a pious act, Herod had the two teachers and their pupils burned alive.

The second event was the announcement by Jewish scholars of that time that they had discovered that 76 generations had passed since the Creation, and there was a well-known prophecy that the Messiah was to deliver Israel from its oppressors in the 77th generation! Messianic hopes came alive again and spread throughout the nation.

Most of the believers in the Messiah, and a good example would be Judas Iscariot, considered the oppressor of the Jews to be Rome's military occupation and control over the people's physical lives. Few believers understood the oppressor to be the possession of the people's spirits and souls by their egoism, materialism, and physicality. The real oppressor that the Messiah was coming to overthrow was *within* the people's hearts and minds.

The third event was when Herod ordered all male babies under two years of age brutally torn from their mothers and killed, in response to the Magi from the East informing him that the stars revealed that the prophesied King of the Jews had recently been born in Judea. Within a year of that horrible act Herod the Great died.

Herod's succession led to factional strife in his family. Shortly before his death, Herod decided against his sons Aristobulus and Antipater and had them executed in 7 and 4 BC, causing the emperor Augustus (emperor from 32 BC to 14 AD) to joke that it was preferable to be Herod's pig (*hus*) than his son (*huios*). Ultimately, the emperor himself divided greater Judea among Herod's remaining sons. Herod Antipas (the beheader of John the Baptist) was to rule Galilee and the east bank of the Jordan as a tetrarch (regional ruler); Philip was to be tetrarch of the Golan Heights in the northeast; and Archelaus became the *ethnarch* (national ruler) of Samaria and Judea. But in 6 AD, Roman governors replaced Archelaus. In 26 AD,

Pontius Pilate became the governor and ruled until 36 AD, covering the entire ministry of both John the Baptist and Jesus Christ. In addition to the ordinary duty of financial administration (mostly tax collection), Pilate was given supreme judicial power to oversee all trials. The official residence of the governor was the palace in Caesarea, where there was a military force of about 3,000 soldiers. These soldiers came down to Jerusalem during feasts, when the city was full of strangers, to provide more security; hence it was then that Pilate had come to Jerusalem at the time of the capture of Jesus. It was the feast of Passover.

Philo of Alexandria described Pilate as inflexible, merciless, and obstinate (*The Legatio ad Gaium*, 38). The Jews hated him and his administration because he was severe (ordering over 100 crucifixions) and showed little consideration for their sensitivities. Standards bearing the image of the emperor Tiberius (14 to 32 AD), which had been set up by Pilate in Jerusalem, caused an uproar that would have ended in a massacre had Pilate not removed them. Later, the Emperor himself ordered Pilate to remove golden shields, which he had set up in Jerusalem in spite of the people's protests. Following these instances, Pilate was anxious that no more negative reports about him reach the emperor. Thus the Gospels and Christians contend that Pilate's role in the crucifixion was minimal, because Pilate wanted to keep the peace. In the apocryphal Gospels there are claims that Pilate actually became a Christian. The Abyssinian Church recognizes him as a saint. They also hold his wife, Claudia Procula, to be a saint because she, too, became a Christian. This belief goes back to the second century and may be found in the Gnostic writings of Origen (Homilies in "Commentaries on St. Matthew," xxxv). Cayce's readings add that the governor's son had been healed by Jesus (Cayce, 324-5); therefore, Pilate was not inclined to harm Jesus. Add to this that Pilate's wife, Claudia, had a dream warning against harming Jesus.

Much of the blame for the crucifixion of Jesus falls on the Sanhedrin, the ruling council of the main body of the Jewish faith, whose temple was the great Temple in Jerusalem. At this time, Essenean Jews had separated themselves from the rule of the Sanhedrin. The Essene lands were in Qumran, and their main temple was on Mt. Carmel. The aristocratic Saducean Jews had been ousted from the Sanhedrin by Herod the Great and therefore had no voice on the council.

The Sanhedrin was a council of 70 elders, all male. However, they were not a homogenous group. Some among them believed that Jesus was indeed a prophet of God, possibly even the expected Messiah. Of course, the High Priest, Caiaphas, did not believe this and drew the majority of the council to his view, resulting in the vote going against Jesus.

Caiaphas and his supporters wanted to consolidate their power. They sought to use Roman power to do so, even against such fellow Jews as the Essenes and Sadducees (Pharisean Jews were on the council). The story goes that after John the Baptist's death, Jesus grew in notoriety, attracting much attention and teaching a message that was touching the people deeply, causing them to change their ways and shift their loyalties. This was not good for the Sanhedrin's power base. Therefore, Caiaphas and his supporters wanted to capture Jesus while he was away from the crowds. They enlisted the help of Judas Iscariot to notify them of Jesus' whereabouts and opportunities to seize him. When Judas informed them that Jesus was in a garden late at night with only a few of his disciples, the soldiers serving the Sanhedrin followed Judas to this garden and arrested Jesus. They brought him before a late-night meeting of the Sanhedrin (probably not the full 70-member council) for trial and judgment.

Some members of the Sanhedrin spoke in support of Jesus, namely Nicodemus, Joseph, Ardemetus, Zxnew, Gamaliel, and a few others (Cayce, 1151-10, 953-6, and others). But the majority voted to condemn Jesus to death for identifying himself so personally and familiarly with God, a blasphemy so evil that it could not be tolerated and was punishable by death. The evidence against Jesus was his own words. When Jesus spoke of God he used the Hebrew word *Abba*, which means something like *Papa*. In the mind of those present, no one was that personally related to God. Jesus also called himself "the son of God," explaining that even the scriptures say that we are all gods, sons and daughters of the Most High (Psalm 82:6). But a portion of the Sanhedrin wanted Jesus dead and his movement crushed. Most of the Jews were not members or even supporters of the Sanhedrin. Matthew 27:20 clearly states that the Jewish crowd before Pilate was coerced by the Sanhedrin: "The chief priests and the elders persuaded the multitudes to ask for Barabbas, and destroy Jesus." As the crowd called for Barabbas, Claudia warned her husband to "have nothing to do with that righteous man, for I have suffered many things this day in a dream because of him." The Gospels say that Pilate washed his hands of the matter and asked the elders and the crowd what they wanted him to do with Jesus, to which they replied, "Crucify him."

Edgar Cayce's reading of the Akashic Record states plainly and simply: "So did the High Priest condemn your Lord! So did those of the Sanhedrin wreak their own purposes upon Him" (Cayce, 262-61). Obviously, both Cayce and historical records reveal that only a small power base of the Jews killed Jesus.

CRUSHING COLLAPSE AND DISPERSION

At the time of Jesus' life, there were several, distinct Jewish groups. There were the Pharisees, Sadducees, Essenes, and

Samaritans in and around Palestine-Judea, and beyond this region were the many Jews of the Diaspora, which had blended with several different cultures. But in the first ten years of the new era (AD), a new zealous spirit was rising in and around the Holy Land. In 6 AD the Zealot's party was founded. They immediately refused to pay taxes to the Romans and advocated the overthrow of Roman rule, because Jews should be led only by God. Since Jesus clearly advocated "rendering unto Caesar that which is Caesar's and unto God that which is God's" (Mark 12:13-17), he would not likely have been a zealot, though at least one of his disciples was, Simon (Luke 6:15, Acts 1:13).

Zealots used guerrilla tactics to further their cause. The *Sicarii* (Assassins) carried daggers (*sica*) and kidnapped or murdered any who had made alliances with the Romans! According to Josephus, it was the Sicarii who made the famous stand against the Romans at Masada (73 AD). Another group, the Covenanters, from Damascus, was a spin-off of the larger group of Pharisees. The Covenanters sought a monastic life, forswearing material goods and sensual gratification, sharing communally all goods and land. They followed in the footsteps of the well-established ascetic Essenes in Qumran and Mt. Carmel. It is important to note here that Therapeutae, an Essene-like Jewish group that flourished in Egypt two centuries earlier, sought knowledge and wisdom through ablutions, ritual purity, prayer, contemplation, and study. But the Essenes in the Palestine area were almost anti-intellectual; knowledge was not their goal. They wanted to simply live a spiritual life in oneness with the forces of Light and God. There are records of the time that indicate that among the people at Qumran were many military activists, yet Essenes as a whole were known to have been pacifists and isolationists. All these groups believed, as did the Gnostics, that the world of matter was evil; spirit was the only true reality and objective.

The spirit that is so identified with Christianity was already latent, if not manifest, in many of the movements within the Judaism of the time. Ideas of apocalyptic change, of an afterlife more important than the current life but affected by how well the current life was lived, the values found in martyrdom, proselytism, monasticism, mysticism, and religious philosophy were all ascending in the minds and hearts of many of the several groups of the Jews at the time of Jesus' birth and ministry. The new doctrine of the Messiah, a Logos ("the Word") as an intermediary between God and the world, laid the foundation for the new movement that became Christianity. In the Dead Sea Scrolls there were clear indications that the "Teacher of Righteousness" would suffer for the sins of humankind. Several groups held the idea that a divinely ordained incarnation was to occur and that this one would take on the sins of the world and through his blood-sacrifice, would counterbalance the force of evil over that of good, both in the greater world and in the little world of each soul.

Under the stress from powerful secular forces occupying the Holy Land, the Jewish population was polarizing between those who simply wanted to practice their faith and those who wanted to overthrow all outside powers. But Rome continued to secularize that Holy Land and even the Temple, and busts of the Roman emperors were around the Holy City. Emperor Caligula demanded that his bust be installed *inside* the Temple! None of the Jews could allow this type of desecration, uniting them in a bloody rebellion from 66 to 73 AD. The Roman general Titus, who later became emperor, brutally crushed the rebellion and in 70 AD and destroyed the great Temple, not leaving one stone unturned, as Jesus had prophesied on the Mount of Olives (Matthew 24:1-2). In 73 AD, the rebellion ended when the *Sicarii* committed mass suicide at Masada rather than submit to Roman rule.

There were smaller rebellions and would-be messiahs in those days. Herodians actually believed that Herod the Great had been the prophesied messiah, and long after his death they were still seeking to reestablish the rule of Herod's descendants over an independent Palestine. Lukuas-Andreas, a Cyrenian messiah-king led a widespread, two-year-long revolt to free Palestine from the Romans (115-117). The messiah, Bar Kokhba, who had the support of one of the greatest rabbis of the time, Akıba, led a three-year-long uprising against Rome (132-135), which resulted in Roman laws against circumcision and public instruction in the Torah. The defeat of Bar Kokhba marked the end of Jewish resistance to Roman rule. Having no longer any national organization or Temple, the Jews began to live and practice their faith in small, autonomous community groups under the guidance of a rabbi. Sacrifice and pilgrimage to the Temple were replaced once again with prayer, study of the Scriptures, and works of faith. Diaspora was now the way of all Jews, even those living in and around Palestine. This period began around 200 AD and continued through to the 1700s. Around the 1700s the Diaspora Jews began to return to the Holy Land with the hope of rebuilding a Jewish homeland. This culminated in the establishment of the State of Israel in 1947.

JERUSALEM AFTER ROME

In 638 the Muslim caliph Umar entered Jerusalem, taking control of the Holy City. Jerusalem is the third holiest city in Islam, after Mecca and Medina. Between 688 and 691, caliph Adb Al-Malik ibn Marwan built the Dome of the Rock on the very spot where the great Temple once stood, the Temple Mount.

The golden-domed monument is the most photographed icon of the Holy City. Moslems believe that the prophet Mohammed ascended to heaven from this very spot. They also believe that this was the place where

Abraham was going to sacrifice his son Isaac, but the Lord gave him a ram instead. The Koran indicates (Nuseibeh 43) that the Dome of the Rock may also commemorate a well-known night journey made by Mohammed while being guided by the archangel Gabriel (the patron angel of the Ishmaelites, the Arabs; Michael is the patron of the Israelites) to the "farthest mosque," which would have been Jerusalem. Here Mohammed met all the prophets, experienced Hell and glimpsed Heaven, where he saw God sitting on His throne.

Except for taxes, these Umayyad caliphs (638-969) usually maintained a liberal policy toward Jews and Christians, but in 969 the Shiite Fatimid caliphs of Egypt took control of the Holy City and destroyed all Christian shrines (Jews do not make shrines). In 1071 the Seljuq Turks (1037-1281, also Muslim) took control of the city and created the famous pilgrim roads for Christians to come and worship in the city again. Eventually, the Christians wanted the Holy City for themselves, and the Crusades began on July 15, 1099, along these same pilgrim roads. From 1099 to 1187 Jerusalem was ruled by the Christians. In 1187, out of Egypt, but of Kurdish origin, arose the powerful Muslim leader Saladin, who recaptured the Holy City and held it against all the onslaughts of the Crusaders. On October 9, 1192, Richard the Lionheart sailed for home, exhausted by his efforts to retake Jerusalem – the Crusades were effectively over. Saladin's successors ruled Jerusalem from Damascus. Christians regained control briefly from 1229 to 1239 and from 1243 to 1244. In 1247 Jerusalem fell once again to the Egyptian Muslims, who held it until 1517, when the mighty Ottoman Empire (1517-1917) rose up and proceeded to conquer much of the Mediterranean lands, all the way to Spain and Morocco. The Ottomans were not descendants of Ishmael, as the Arabs were, but they were an ethnic people of Asian origin, yet they were Muslims. In 1832 Muhammad Ali

Pasha of Egypt and his son Ibrahim took over Jerusalem and governed until 1840. In 1838 the British consulate opened in the Holy City, helping Jewish immigration to increase dramatically. In 1917 British troops entered the city and placed it under their administration. In 1947 the British signed an agreement with the Jews to establish the State of Israel in Palestine. So many riots occurred between the Jews and the Arabs that in 1948 the city was divided between them. In June of 1967 Israeli troops entered and occupied the Old City (which includes the Temple Mount and the Dome of the Rock) in what was called the Six-Day War. Tensions between the descendants of these two sons of Abraham – Ishmael (Arabs) and Isaac (Jews) – continued.

A Broader View

Chapter Two
The Incarnation of Jesus Christ

Beyond the Gospels, there are few historical documents that provide evidence and detail to Jesus' existence. The most famous and widely accepted as authentic comes from the writings of Flavius Josephus, a historian who lived from 37 to 100 AD and wrote the following description of Jesus in his *Antiquities Of The Jews*, Book 18, Chapter 3:

"Now there was about this time Jesus, a wise man, if it be lawful to call him a man; for he was a doer of wonderful works, a teacher of such men as receive the truth with pleasure. He drew over to him both many of the Jews and many of the Gentiles. He was Christ [Greek for Messiah]. And when Pilate, at the suggestion of the principal men amongst us, had condemned him to the cross, those that loved him at the first did not forsake him; for he appeared to them alive again the third day, as the divine prophets had foretold these and ten thousand other wonderful things concerning him. And the tribe of Christians, so named from him, are not extinct at this day."

In Book 20, Chapter 200, Josephus wrote about the stoning of Jesus' brother in 62 AD, including this line that clearly indicates the existence of both Jesus and his brother: "James, the brother of Jesus, who was called Christ...."

There are more of these non-biblical sources, but they have limited scholarly support for their authenticity. One is a letter that appears to have been written by

Pontius Pilate to Caesar. In it Pilate describes Jesus: "His golden colored hair and beard gave to his appearance a celestial aspect. He appeared to be about 30 years of age. Never have I seen a sweeter or more serene countenance." I can't image Pilate writing *celestial* and *sweet* as a description of one of his defendants unless he, Pilate, was indeed a sympathizer with Jesus and his message, as some texts suggest.

Another description comes from a Roman official in Judea at the time of Jesus named Lucius Lentulus, circa 30 AD. It appears in a Latin manuscript, MS 22, in the library of the University of Chicago. The manuscript appears to have been written in 1466-1469 in Europe, probably Italy. In some other medieval manuscripts, the letter is described as being from "Publius Lentulus, Governor of Judea, to the Roman Senate." Since there never was a governor of Palestine called Lentulus, the letter is suspect. There was, however, a Publius Cornelius Lentulus (both a father and a son) mentioned by Cicero, who lived in the first century before Christ. There was also a Lucius Lentulus who held the office of consul in Rome, not Judea. Perhaps the letter is from this Lentulus, while he was visiting Judea. We will never know for sure. Here's what the letter says:

"There lives at this time in Judea a man of singular virtue whose name is Jesus Christ, whom the barbarians esteem as a prophet, but his followers love and adore him as the offspring of the immortal God. He calls back the dead from the graves and heals all sorts of diseases with a word or touch. He is a tall man, well-shaped, and of an amiable and reverend aspect; his hair of a color that can hardly be matched, falling into graceful curls, waving about and very agreeable crouching upon his shoulders, parted on the crown of the head, running as a stream to the front after fashion of the Nazarites. His forehead high, large and imposing; his cheeks without spot or wrinkle, beautiful with a lovely red; his nose and mouth formed with exquisite symmetry; his beard, and of a color suitable to his hair, reaching below his chin and parted in the middle like a fork; his eyes bright blue, clear and serene. Look innocent, dignified, manly and mature. In proportion of body most perfect, and captivating; his arms and hands delectable to behold. He rebukes with majesty, councils with mildness. His whole address whether in word or deed, being eloquent and grave. No man has seen him laugh, yet his manners are exceedingly pleasant, but he has wept frequently in the presence of men. He is temperate, modest and wise. A man for his extraordinary beauty and perfection, surpassing the children of men in every sense."

Of solid authenticity are documents from later periods, long after Jesus' incarnation, giving evidence to his life and influence. For example, Roman historian Tacitus wrote in 110 AD his account of the persecution of Christians under the emperor Nero, which occurred at the same time as the burning of Rome in 64 AD. Nero blamed the burning on the Christians, who were already hated by the Romans. Tacitus wrote: "Their name is derived from Christ, whom the procurator Pontius Pilate had executed in the reign of Tiberius." Tacitus explained that the "pernicious superstition" to which Christ had given rise to in Judea had spread far and wide, even to Rome. Tacitus never uses the name "Jesus," only "Christ," when referring to the founder of the faith. We know that very early the followers of Jesus began referring to him by the formal name Christ, which is derived from the Greek word for messiah, "christos," meaning the same as the Hebrew word *mashiach* (first used in Daniel 9:25-26 by the angel Gabriel), which is transliterated to *messiah*. The word literally means "anointed one." Tacitus' writings give support to the existence and ultimate sentence, crucifixion, of an individual in Palestine known as Christ, who began a movement that gained widespread influence some eighty years after his execution.

A letter, written in 111 AD, by Pliny the Younger, the governor of Asia Minor (modern Turkey), asks Emperor Trajan (97-117 AD) how Pliny should deal with Christians. It describes the Christians as adherents to a superstition who sing hymns to Christ "as to a god."

In a biography of Emperor Claudius (41-54 AD), Roman historian Suetonius wrote that in 49 AD the emperor "expelled the Jews from Rome, who had on the instigation of Chrestus continually caused disturbances." These disturbances may have been due to the Jews in Rome becoming either angered or inspired by a Christian agitator named Chrestus. Or Chrestus may also be a Latin variation of the name Christ, though *Christi* is the proper Latin equivalent of the Greek word *Christos*. Emperor Claudius' expulsion of the Jews from Rome is actually mentioned in the Bible, in Acts 18:2.

In the Talmud, a handbook of Jewish law, lore, and teachings, Jesus (*Yeshu* in Hebrew) is described as being born the illegitimate son of a Roman soldier called Panther, and that he practiced magic, ridiculed the wise, seduced and stirred up the people, gathered five disciples about him, and was hanged on the eve of the Passover (in those days *hanged* meant crucified).

The most detailed information of Jesus comes from the biblical testaments: Gospels, Epistles, and the Revelation. In addition to these, there are many other Christian manuscripts and documents beyond the New Testament.

The activities surrounding Jesus' birth, though initially only known to a few within the family's inner circle, were profound, indicating a rare incarnation was about to happen. Jesus' mother, Mary, was visited by the angel Gabriel, who informed her of what was about to happen to her, and the angel's promise was confirmed when Mary came into the presence of her cousin Elizabeth, who was already pregnant with John the Baptist. Here are the passages:

> The angel Gabriel was sent from God to a city of Galilee, named Nazareth, to a virgin pledged to be married to a man whose name was Joseph, of the house of David. The virgin's name was Mary. Having come in, the angel said to her, "Rejoice, you highly favored one! The Lord is with you. Blessed are you among women!" But when she saw him, she was greatly troubled at the saying, and considered what kind of salutation this might be. The angel said to her, "Don't be afraid, Mary, for you have found favor with God. Behold, you will conceive in your womb, and bring forth a son, and will call his name 'Jesus.' He will be great, and will be called the Son of the Most High. The Lord God will give him the throne of his father, David, and he will reign over the house of Jacob forever. There will be no end to his kingdom." Mary said to the angel, "How can this be, seeing I am a virgin?" The angel answered her, "The Holy Spirit will come upon you, and the power of the Most High will overshadow you. Therefore also the holy one who is born from you will be called the Son of God. Behold, Elizabeth, your relative, also has conceived a son in her old age; and this is the sixth month with her who was called barren. For everything spoken by God is possible." Mary said, "Behold, the handmaid of the Lord; be it to me according to your word." The angel departed from her. Mary arose in those days and went into the hill country with haste, into a city of Judah, and entered into the house of Zacharias and greeted Elizabeth. It happened, when Elizabeth heard Mary's greeting, that the baby leaped in her womb, and Elizabeth

was filled with the Holy Spirit. She called out with a loud voice, and said, "Blessed are you among women, and blessed is the fruit of your womb! Why am I so favored, that the mother of my Lord should come to me? For behold, when the voice of your greeting came into my ears, the baby leaped in my womb for joy! Blessed is she who believed, for there will be a fulfillment of the things which have been spoken to her from the Lord!" Mary said, "My soul magnifies the Lord. My spirit has rejoiced in God my Savior, for he has looked at the humble state of his handmaid. For behold, from now on, all generations will call me blessed. For he who is mighty has done great things for me. Holy is his name. His mercy is for generations of generations on those who fear him. He has shown strength with his arm. He has scattered the proud in the imagination of their heart. He has put down princes from their thrones; and has exalted the lowly. He has filled the hungry with good things. He has sent the rich away empty. He has given help to Israel, his servant, that he might remember mercy, as he spoke to our fathers, to Abraham and his seed forever." (Luke 1:26-55)

Joseph, Jesus' earthly father, also received a message from an angel that conveyed the specialness of this coming child. Here are those passages in Matthew 1:20-24:

Mary, was engaged to Joseph, but before they came together, she was found pregnant by the Holy Spirit. Joseph, her husband, being a righteous man, and not willing to make her a public example, intended to put her away secretly. But when he thought about these things, behold, an angel of the Lord appeared to him in a dream, saying, "Joseph, son of David, don't be afraid to take to yourself Mary, your wife, for that which is conceived in her is of the Holy Spirit. She shall bring forth a son. You shall call his name Jesus, for it is he who shall save his people from their sins." Now all this has happened, that it might be fulfilled which was spoken by the Lord through the prophet [Isaiah], saying, "Behold, the virgin shall be with child, And shall bring forth a son. They shall call his name *Emmanuel*; Which is, being interpreted, 'God with us.'" Joseph arose from his sleep, and did as the angel of the Lord commanded him.

As mentioned earlier, the Revelation identifies Jesus as "the root and the offspring of David" (Rev. 22-16). He is even referred to as "Son of David" (Mark 10:48). The Gospels attempt to show that this linkage is not simply esoteric but physical. Matthew's Gospel opens this way: "The book of the Genealogy of Jesus Christ, the son of David, the son of Abraham," and then proceeds to trace the lineage of Joseph, Jesus' earthly father, back through David to Abraham. In Luke's Gospel, 3:23-38, we also find Jesus' genealogy, but this one traces it all the way back through David and Abraham to Adam.

Another connection is that Jesus' parents were of the city of Bethlehem, which was David's hometown. This is why Mary and Joseph had to leave their residence in the town of Nazareth, in the hills of Galilee, to journey back to Bethlehem to register for the taxation. The emperor had ordered all to return to their place of origin to register. Bethlehem was the Davidic family's place of origin. As the Gospels tell the story, while Joseph and Mary were in Bethlehem, Jesus was born, thus making his birthplace another tie-in with David.

Though the Gospels tell us that his birth was modest, it was not without fanfare and notice. Three Magi (plural of Latin *magus*; Greek *magoi*, meaning "magician," perhaps referring to their ability to read the stars) journeyed from the East looking for a prophesied child, born at this time and location. Psalm 71:10 may have actually prophesied the coming of the Magi and given a description of them: "The kings of Tharsis and the islands shall offer presents; the kings of the Arabians and of Saba shall bring him gifts; and all the kings of the earth shall adore him." Historically, these Magi are believed to have been a remnant of an outlawed priestly caste of the Pre-Persian Medes. The original lands of the Medes were estimated to have been from the Caspian Sea to India, engulfing modern Turkey, Iraq, Armenia, and Persia. When Darius became king of Persia in 521 BC, this priestly caste was outlawed, though secretly their guidance continued to be sought by the Persian leaders for hundreds of years. This means that the modern Christian belief that they were kings is not supported by the historical record, though they were "kingly," meaning rich and accompanied by an entourage that would have attracted much attention and wonder. They either were brought before the king of Judea, Herod the Great, concerning the reason for their presence in his country, or wisely requested an audience with him before he commanded it. As we know, once Herod heard of their reason for coming, he ordered the death of all male children under the age of two in an attempt to kill the prophesied "King of the Jews."

Herod's order to kill all male babies under two years of age forced the Holy Family to flee to Egypt for safety. Luke's Gospel contradicts Matthew's, having the family first return to Nazareth after the birth (Luke 2:39), rather than immediately fleeing directly from Bethlehem to Egypt , as Matthew tells it (Matt. 2:13-14). The family would not have been in Egypt more than four or five years because Herod the Great died in 4 AD, and his kingdom was divided among his sons by the Roman Emperor. His son Herod Antipas became the regional ruler of Galilee, which included the town of Nazareth, Jesus' childhood home from about five years of age. The Bible records that Joseph received a dream message that he could take his child back into the lands of Israel because those who sought his death were dead (Matt. 2:19-20).

In Nazareth, Jesus would have been raised to study the Torah, obey the Law, pray, and attend the synagogue. He and his family would have made pilgrimages to the Temple in Jerusalem, as was customary. In fact, in Luke we are told that Jesus and his family went to the Jerusalem Temple every year at Passover. Luke records it this way in 2:40-52:

> The child was growing, and was becoming strong in spirit, being filled with wisdom, and the grace of God was upon him. His parents went every year to Jerusalem at the feast of the Passover. When he was twelve years old, they went up to Jerusalem according to the custom of the feast, and when they had fulfilled the days, as they were returning, the boy Jesus stayed behind in Jerusalem. Joseph and his mother didn't know it, supposing him to be in the company, they went a day's journey, and they looked for him among their relatives and acquaintances. When they didn't find him, they returned to Jerusalem, looking for him. It happened after three days they found him in the Temple, sitting in the midst of the teachers, both listening to them, and asking them questions. All who heard him were amazed at his understanding and his answers. When they saw him, they were astonished, and his mother said to him, "Son, why have you treated us this way? Behold, your father and I were anxiously looking for you." He said to them, "Why were you looking for me? Didn't you know that I must be in my Father's house?" They didn't understand the saying which he spoke to them. And he went down with them, and came to Nazareth. He was subject to them, and his mother

kept all these sayings in her heart. And Jesus increased in wisdom and stature, and in favor with God and men.

RETURN OF THE MAGI

According to Edgar Cayce's reading of the Akashic Record, the Magi returned several times to Galilee to visit the Holy Family and keep up with the progress of the boy's growth. They returned at least five times, and not always the same Magi. Cayce says, "They came from Persia, India, Egypt [initially], and also from Chaldea, Gobi, and what is now the Indo or Tao land." According to these readings, at the fifth visit, when Jesus had become "of age" (which in those days would have been 12 years old), the Magi took him from Jerusalem to their temples for training and testing. These temples were in Persia (modern day Iran), India, and Egypt (Cayce 2067-7).

Cayce explained that the three Wise Men, as they are also called, and their gifts "represent in the metaphysical sense the three phases of man's experience in materiality: gold, the material; frankincense, the ether or ethereal; myrrh, the healing force as brought with same; or body, mind, soul." In these readings, Egypt was the source for the gold. But in two different readings Cayce gives the source of the incense to Persia in one (#1908, a Persian Wise Man named *Achlar*) and to India in another (#256, an Indian Wise Man named *Ashtueil*). Perhaps, in one of the many visits, the Wise Man from Persia brought the frankincense, while in another visit, the one from India brought it. In those days, myrrh came from East India. Myrrh was used in the holy oil of the Jews and the *Kyphi* of the Egyptians. In the initial visitation by the Magi, it is likely that the myrrh came from India, the frankincense from Persia, and the gold from Egypt. Therefore, using Cayce's correlations, we could conclude that ancient Egypt represented the material phase, ancient Persia the ethereal phase, and ancient India the healing phase of human experience.

As to the young Jesus' training and testing, the readings say that he first went to Persia. There he would have been trained and tested according to the ways of Zoroastrianism, from the sacred books *Avesta* and the *Gathas* ("Older Hymns"). This faith is at the same time monotheistic and dualistic: teaching that there is only one God but two distinct forces battling for the hearts and minds of God's children: good and evil. Each soul must choose which of these forces it will adhere to, using its free will to do so. Those following the path of evil are called "The Followers of the Lie." Despite this battle, there is an underlying optimism in Zoroastrianism because it is understood that God and Good are destined from the start to win the battle.

The Gathas teaches that Wise God (*Ahura Mazda*) is the father of seven "Good Spirits" (*Amesha Spentas*), which help guide those who seek to align with Good; they are these: 1. The Holy Spirit; 2. Truthful Justice; 3. Righteous Thinking; 4. Devotion; 5. The "Desirable Dominion," which is a content state of peace and harmony; 6. Wholeness; and 7. Immortality. The first Good Spirit, "Holy Spirit," is an exact, literal translation of the Persian term *Spenta Mainyu*, which indicates that Jesus' later teachings about the importance of the Holy Spirit may have been known to his soul as far back as the sixth century BC and relearned during his sojourn in Persia. Zoroastrianism also includes teachings that there will be a judgment of the soul at death and a resurrection of souls at the end times, when the "Desirable Dominion" is established forever.

After Persia, the Cayce readings say young Jesus went to India and was there for three years, studying under a teacher named *Arcahia*. He attended many schools in India, including the large ones in Jagannath and Benares.

In India he would have been trained and tested according to ancient Hinduism, which would be found in the sacred texts of the *Vedas, Upanishads,* and the *Bhagavad-Gita* ("The Lord's Song," circa 200 BC). He would have learned about Brahman and Atman. Brahman is an uncreated, eternal, infinite, transcendent, and all-embracing essence, which includes both being and non-being. It is the only, true reality. Atman is the Self, the Logos, and the central consciousness of Beingness. In Western terms, it is the great "I AM" and is reflected in all the little "I ams." Atman gives self-consciousness to all beings. Atman is personal. Yet Atman exists within Brahman. Brahman is impersonal. Brahman is the One, the Whole, within which and through which everything exists. Brahman is also expressed in a Trinity: Brahma (the Creator, a personification of Brahman), Vishnu (the Preserver), and Shiva (the Destroyer). Jesus' teachings about the Trinity have some degree of harmony with ancient Hindu concepts.

Like Zoroastrianism, ancient Hinduism teaches that there is a battle raging between the good gods (*devas*) and the demoniac antigods (*asuras*). The cosmos (*sat*) is naturally governed by order and truth but is always in danger of being damaged or even destroyed by the powers of chaos (*asat*). During his time in India young Jesus would have also learned about reincarnation and karma.

The Cayce readings indicate that Jesus did as much teaching as learning and that much of what he experienced was in the form of testings rather than initiations, with the exception of his time in Egypt, where initiation was the primary experience. The "testings" were mostly conversations with the teachers and priests of these lands, just as he had experienced in the Temple in Jerusalem prior to departing. In *The Aquarian Gospel of Jesus Christ* by Levi, a writer who also received his information from the Akashic Records, or what he called "God's Book of

Remembrance," we find some detail on one incident which occurred during Jesus' time in India that may be an example of these testings. It is in chapter 29 of *The Aquarian Gospel* and goes like this:

> Among Benares' temple priests was one, a guest, Ajainan, from Lahore. By merchant men Ajainin heard about the Jewish boy, about his words of wisdom, and he girt himself and journeyed from Lahore that he might see the boy, and hear him speak. The Brahmic priests did not accept the truth that Jesus brought, and they were angered much by what he said at the Udraka feast. But they had never seen the boy, and they desired much to hear him speak, and they invited him to be a temple guest. But Jesus said to them, "The light is most abundant, and it shines for all; if you would see the light come to the light. If you would hear the message that the Holy One has given me to give to men, come unto me." Now, when the priests were told what Jesus said they were enraged. Ajainin did not share their wrath, and he sent forth another messenger with costly gifts to Jesus at the farmer's home; he sent this message with the gifts: "I pray you master, listen to my words; The Brahmic law forbids that any priest shall go into the home of any one of low estate; but you can come to us; And I am sure these priests will gladly hear you speak. I pray that you will come and dine with us this day." And Jesus said, "The Holy One regards all men alike; the dwelling of my host is good enough for any council of the sons of men. If pride of cast keeps you away, you are not worthy of the light. My Father-God does not regard the laws of man. Your presents I return; you cannot buy the knowledge of the

Lord with gold, or precious gifts." These words of Jesus angered more and more the priests, and they began to plot and plan how they might drive him from the land. Ajainin did not join with them in plot and plan; he left the temple in the night, and sought the home where Jesus dwelt. And Jesus said, "There is no night where shines the sun; I have no secret messages to give; in light all secrets are revealed." Ajainin said, "I came from faraway Lahore, that I might learn about this ancient wisdom, and this kingdom of the Holy One of which you speak. Where is the kingdom? where the king? Who are the subjects? what its laws?" And Jesus said, "This kingdom is not far away, but man with mortal eyes can see it not; it is within the heart. You need not seek the king in earth, or sea, or sky; he is not there, and yet is everywhere. He is the Christ of God; is universal love. The gate of this dominion is not high, and he who enters it must fall down on his knees. It is not wide, and none can carry carnal bundles through. The lower self must be transmuted into spirit-self; the body must be washed in living streams of purity." Ajainin asked, "Can I become a subject of this king?" And Jesus said, "You are yourself a king, and you may enter through the gate and be a subject of the King of kings. But you must lay aside your priestly robes; must cease to serve the Holy One for gold; must give your life, and all you have, in willing service to the sons of men." And Jesus said no more; Ajainin went his way; and while he could not comprehend the truth that Jesus spoke, he saw what he had never seen before. The realm of faith he never had explored; but in his heart the seeds of faith and universal brotherhood had found good soil. And as he journeyed to his home he seemed to sleep, to pass through darkest night, and when he woke the Sun of Righteousness had arisen; he had found the king. Now, in Benares Jesus tarried many days and taught.

From this account we can see that young Jesus was already experiencing the challenges of authorities, traditions, and prejudices, which he would also find in Judea during his coming ministry.

Since Cayce identifies one of the Wise Men as coming from "Tao Land," young Jesus would have learned about Taoism. Along with Confucianism, Taoism was one of the chief religions of ancient China. Taoism conveys a positive, active attitude toward the occult and metaphysical, in contrast to the agnostic, pragmatic Confucian traditions of social duty and austerity. The sacred texts of Taoism are *Tao-te Ching* (written by Lao-tzu), the *Chuang-tzu*, and the *Lieh-tzu*. Tao means "Way," referring to the way to fulfillment and immortality. According to Lao-tzu there is a Tao that is named and can be studied and practiced, but then there is a Tao that is unnamed and can only be experienced through an ecstasy that transcends normal reality. Taoism teaches that all multiplicity is returning, at least in consciousness, if not ultimately in reality, to a former oneness that it enjoyed before the creation. This can be mystically achieved in a moment of deep stillness, when all beingness returns to nonbeing, all action to nonaction. In Taoism there are again two forces in the world: those that disperse and those that unite; one of these sees only the manyness, the other sees the oneness. Yin and Yang would have been shown as two interwoven principles that manifest themselves in the separated external world but unite in the internal place of stillness.

Certainly in India and under the influence of those from Tao Land, young Jesus would have learned to meditate, transcending normal consciousness to experience the peace, oneness, and ecstasy of reunion with the Source of Life.

In chapter 36 of *The Aquarian Gospel* we have this depiction of young Jesus' time in Tao Land:

> In Lassa of Tibet there was a master's temple, rich in manuscripts of ancient lore. The Indian sage had read these manuscripts, and he revealed to Jesus many of the secret lessons they contained; but Jesus wished to read them for himself. Now, Meng-ste, greatest sage of all the farther East, was in this temple of Tibet. The path across Emodus heights was difficult; but Jesus started on his way, and Vidyapati sent with him a trusted guide. And Vidyapati sent a message to Meng-ste, in which he told about the Hebrew sage, and spoke for him a welcome by the temple priests. Now, after many days, and perils great, the guide and Jesus reached the Lassa temple in Tibet. And Meng-ste opened wide the temple doors, and all the priests and masters gave a welcome to the Hebrew sage. And Jesus had access to all the sacred manuscripts, and, with the help of Meng- ste, read them all. And Meng-ste often talked with Jesus of the coming age, and of the sacred service best adapted to the people of the age. In Lassa Jesus did not teach. When he finished all his studies in the temple schools he journeyed toward the West. In many villages he tarried for a time and taught. At last he reached the pass, and in the Ladak city, Leh, he was received with favor by the monks, the merchants, and the men of low estate. And in the monastery he abode, and taught; and then he sought the common people in the marts of trade; and there he taught. Not far away a woman lived, whose infant son was sick nigh unto death. The doctors had declared,

"There is no hope; the child must die." The woman heard that Jesus was a teacher sent from God, and she believed that he had power to heal her son. And so she clasped the dying infant in her arms and ran with haste and asked to see the man of God. When Jesus saw her faith he lifted up his eyes to heaven and said, "My Father-God, let power divine overshadow me, and let the Holy Breath fill full this child that it may live." And in the presence of the multitude he laid his hand upon the child and said, "Good woman you are blest; your faith has saved your son." And then the child was well. The people were astonished and they said, "This surely is the Holy One made flesh, for man alone cannot a fever thus and save a child from death." Then many of the people brought their sick, and Jesus spoke the Word, and they were healed. Among the Ladaks Jesus tarried many days; he taught them how to heal; how sins are blotted out, and how to make on earth a heaven of joy.

After Persia, India, and the Tao Land, young Jesus, according to Cayce, spent the rest of his time in Egypt, being trained and tested in Heliopolis (modern-day East Cairo) but taking his most significant initiation in Giza, inside the Great Pyramid. The readings say that John the Baptist was also there but in a different class. Cayce says that the "unifying of the teachings of many lands was brought together in Egypt; for that was the center from which there was to be the radial activity of influence in the Earth ... until the new cycle begins" (2067-7). This "new cycle" is beginning now, in our time, and will lead to the much anticipated New Age, according to the Cayce readings.

In Egypt Jesus would have again found the theme of the Trinity: Ra, the Creator; Osiris, the Preserver and Judge; and Horus, the Savior. He would have again learned of the struggle between Good and Evil. He would have learned about the feminine and masculine forces that appear separate but actually compose a united whole in the higher state of consciousness. He would have learned about powerful feminine goddesses that helped save humanity from evil: Isis, Nephthys, Maat, Hathor, and others.

Cayce says that young Jesus reached the training level of priest in Egypt, and in the readings imply that he broke the King's Chamber sarcophagus during an initiation, as he overcame the power of death. This was apparently a foreshadowing of his victory later at the resurrection: "For, read ye, 'He was also crucified in Egypt'" (Cayce 315-4). This would seem to be a comment on his initiation in Egypt as being like a crucifixion, a dying to self in order to resurrect as a result of making oneself in harmony and oneness with God, the source of all life. Another reading states: "There should be the reminding that, though He bowed under the burden of the Cross, though His blood was shed, though He entered into the tomb – through that power, that ability, that love as manifested in Himself among His fellow men He broke the bonds of death, proclaiming in that act that THERE IS NO DEATH when the individual, the soul, has and does put its trust in Him." (Cayce 5749-13)

In chapter 47 of *The Aquarian Gospel*, we have this account of Jesus' return to Egypt:

> Jesus came to Egypt land and all was well. He tarried not upon the coast; he went at once to Zoan, home of Elihu and Salome, who five and twenty years before had taught his mother in their sacred school. And there was joy when met these three. When last the son of Mary saw these sacred groves he was a babe; And now a man grown strong by buffeting of every kind; a teacher who had stirred the multitudes in many lands. And Jesus told the

aged teachers all about his life; about his journeying in foreign lands; about the meetings with the masters and about his kind receptions by the multitudes. Elihu and Salome heard his story with delight; they lifted up their eyes to heaven and said, "Our Father-God, let now thy servants go in peace, for we have seen the glory of the Lord; And we have talked with him, the messenger of love, and of the covenant of peace on earth, good will to men. Through him shall all the nations of the earth be blest; through him, Emmanuel" (meaning, *God is among men*). And Jesus stayed in Zoan many days; and then went forth unto the city of the sun, that men call Heliopolis, and sought admission to the temple of the sacred brotherhood. The council of the brotherhood convened, and Jesus stood before the hierophant; he answered all the questions that were asked with clearness and with power. The hierophant exclaimed, "Rabboni of the rabbinate, why come you here? Your wisdom is the wisdom of the gods; why seek for wisdom in the halls of men?" And Jesus said, "In every way of earth-life I would walk; in every hall of learning I would sit; the heights that any man has gained, these I would gain; What any man has suffered I would meet, that I may know the griefs, the disappointments and the sore temptations of my brother man; that I may know just how to succor those in need. I pray you, brothers, let me go into your dismal crypts; and I would pass the hardest of your tests." The master said, "Take then the vow of secret brotherhood." And Jesus took the vow of secret brotherhood. Again the master spoke; he said, "The greatest heights are gained by those who reach the greatest depths; and you shall reach the greatest depths."

The Aquarian Gospel records seven trials or tests that Jesus went through in his initiation into the Egyptian mystery school. They were these: 1. the test of Sincerity, in which victory over deceit was achieved; 2. the test of Justice; in which victory over "the phantoms of prejudice and treachery" were achieved; 3. the test of Faith, in which victory over the seduction of earthly wealth, honor, and fame were achieved; 4. the test of Philanthropy or Charity, in which victory over self-gratification was achieved; 5. the test of Heroism, in which victory over fear was achieved; 6. the test of Divine Love, in which victory over getting lost in carnal love was achieved; and 7. the test of Life in the Chamber of Death, in which Death no longer meant the end of one's true self, and consciousness of that true self lives beyond the physical body. Cayce's readings describe this last test as being an actual death of the body in the sarcophagus for a significant duration, becoming conscious in the worlds beyond this one, and then a return to resurrect the body and recall the whole process consciously. Whereas Levi's account is much more a mental wrestling with human perspectives on death.

There are some non-Akashic sources for tales of young Jesus' journeys. And though they are questioned by some, they are worth presenting here. The first is Nicolas Notovitch who traveled throughout India, Tibet, and Afghanistan in the 1880s and wrote that while he was recovering from an injury at the Buddhist monastery Himis, in Ledak (then in the Western region of Tibet but today is in the northernmost part of India), he was shown a copy of a manuscript titled *The Life of Saint Issa. Issa*, Notovitch came to understand, was a Buddhist equivalent of the name Jesus. He was told that the manuscript was about a "saint" from the West who had been revered by Hindus and Buddhists. He managed to have the manuscript read to him aloud, in translation, of course. To his amazement, it contained the whole story of Jesus' life, from twelve years of age until thirty. Notovitch said that the monks told him that the original of this copy was located in the monastery on Mt. Marbour, near Lhasa, with other copies at several of the country's other major monasteries. After the publication of his book in 1894, *The Unknown Life of Jesus Christ*, Notovitch came under much criticism. Orientalist Max Müller, editor of *Sacred Books of the East* series, argued that such an honored work as Notovitch described would surely have been included in the canon of Tibetan books, the *Kanjur* and the *Tanjur*. But it wasn't.

Notovitch's manuscript (reprinted in chapter six of this book) contains an amazing story of the journeys of young Jesus to many of India's classical centers of spiritual thought and practice. Janet Bock and her husband, Richard, traveled to India to retrace the young Jesus' journey as Notovitch had revealed it. Bock's book on their journeys came out in 1980, titled *The Jesus Mystery of the Lost Years and Unknown Travels*.

Thirty-five years after Notovitch, Swami Abhedananda went to Himis in 1922 and saw the manuscript and wrote about it in his Bengali book of travels, *Kashmiri O Tibbetti*, meaning "Journey to Kashmir and Tibet." Swami Abhedananda later wrote another book titled, *Was Christ a Yogi?* In this book the Swami wrote that Christ was more than a yogi and believed that his God was also the God of Hinduism, Jainism, and Buddhism.

Nicholas Roerich, a mystic painter, visited Central Asia in search of the lost city of Shambhala and other mysteries. He, too, visited Himis. In 1925, he recorded what he claimed were extracts of popular tales about Saint Issa as well as related material from a 1500-year-old Tibetan manuscript. Some question his findings, based on the age of this manuscript being nearly four hundred years after the events it supposedly records. Of course, a Bible today is a manuscript recording events that occurred two thousand years ago yet is no less valued as representative of the original story.

In 1939 Dr. Elisabeth Caspari, a member of the Mazdaznan sect, associated with Zoroastrianism, journeyed into Tibet with some female friends and attended a festival at the Himis monastery. One day during their stay, she reports that the librarian and two other monks showed the ladies three Buddhist books made of sheets of parchment, sandwiched between two pieces of wood, and wrapped in brocades. The librarian told the women that these books say your Jesus was here.

Unfortunately, no one brought forth anything that resembles a genuine Tibetan manuscript containing the story of Saint Issa. Since 1947 Tibet and its monasteries have been under the control of Communist China. Therefore, the legend and the Tibetan manuscripts remain a fascinating, unsubstantiated story.

THE FORERUNNER – JOHN THE BAPTIST

Intimately connected with the story of Jesus is the story of John the Baptist, who, as we know, is the son of Elizabeth and Zechariah (some translations render his name as Zacharias). Zechariah was a priest serving in the great Temple in Jerusalem. Elizabeth was the cousin of Jesus' mother. John was born a few months before Jesus and therefore would have had to have been sent out of the land to avoid Herod's death order to all males under two years of age. It is likely that only he and his mother fled to Egypt, because his father, being an active priest in the Temple, would not have been able to be gone out of the country for a few years. Sadly, John's father was murdered by the Sanhedrin when they discovered his ties to the Essenes. John's mother dies when he is only twelve. In Matthew 3, we learn that John becomes an ascetic nomad whose diet (locusts and wild honey), dress (camel's hair and leather), and message ("Repent, for the Kingdom of Heaven is at hand!") attracted many who were seeking repentance and renewal. Matthew's Gospel identifies John as the one spoken of in Isaiah 40:3-5, "A voice cries: 'In the wilderness prepare the way of the Lord, make straight in the desert a highway for our God. Every valley shall be lifted up, and every mountain and hill be made low; the uneven ground shall become level, and the rough places a plain. And the glory of the Lord shall be revealed, and all flesh shall see it together, for the mouth of the Lord has spoken.'"

John was certainly a voice crying in the wilderness. His ministry was not among the people and their towns, synagogues, or the Temple, but in the Judean desert and the Jordan steppes. Yet, from these remote areas his voice and message carried far, drawing many to hear him and receive his baptism, and drawing the wrath of those in authority whom he often chastised. Historian Josephus characterizes him as a moralizer with a washing ritual, which reflects the opinion of the authorities of that time.

But the Gospel of John identifies him as the prophesied forerunner of the Messiah. This prophecy is found in Malachi 4:5, "Behold, I will send you Elijah the prophet before the great and terrible day when the Lord comes." John's manner and appearance reflects the spirit and style that were so naturally Elijah. Elijah first appears in 1 Kings 17. He is identified as a Tishbite, meaning that he was from Tishbi, a place in Upper Galilee, which is mentioned in the Jewish apocryphal book of Tobit. He journeyed from Tishbi into Gilead, a mountainous region east of Jordan. However, the historian Josephus supposes that Tishbi was some place in the land of Gilead (Ant. 8:13, 2). It has been identified by some with *el-Ishtib*, a place some twenty-two miles south of the Sea of Galilee, among the mountains of Gilead. Whatever the case, all of this area is wilderness, and Elijah is guided, as is John, by God to live in the wilderness and deliver His message to the rulers in the surrounding towns. God instructs Elijah to live by "the brook Cherith, that is before the Jordan. It shall be, that you shall drink of the brook; and I have commanded the ravens to feed you there." (1 Kings 1:1-6) The ravens bring Elijah bread in the morning and the evening. Elijah is directed to go to the Jewish king Ahab, who has wrongfully married a daughter not of Israel, Jezebel, and has built altars to her god, Baal. The parallels between this story of Elijah and John's experiences with Herod Antipas and his unlawful wife, Herodias, are extraordinary. When Jesus' disciples ask him why Elijah did not come before the Messiah, twice Jesus explains that he did indeed come first but no one recognized him. The first incident came while John was in prison. Jesus was speaking about John's greatness and then said in Matthew 11:14-15: "And if you care to accept it, he is Elijah, who was to come. He who has ears to hear, let him hear." The second time was after the Transfiguration, in Matthew 17:12-13; Jesus explains: "Elijah is coming and will restore all things; but I say to you, that Elijah already came, and they did not recognize him, but did to him whatever they wished.' Then the disciples understood that He had spoken to them about John the Baptist." John was the soul and spirit of Elijah reincarnated. Curiously, Herodias, the one who had John beheaded, may have been the return of Jezebel, who hated Elijah and swore that she would get even with him for killing her prophets of Baal (1 Kings 19:2). Head chopping would not have been new to Herodias' soul, for, as Jezebel, she had so many heads of the prophets of Jehovah that Obadiah had to "hide a hundred prophets in caves" to keep her from finding them too. Some believe that Elijah karmically "lost his head" when he exceeded his God-given assignment of proving the true God's presence to the people and priests of Baal, when, after proving it by calling down fire from heaven to the altar, he then decided on his own to slay all the Baal priests (1 Kings 18:40) –

something God had not requested. Subsequently, Elisha replaces Elijah as God's prophet, because Elijah fears for his life. So often in our zeal to spread the light, we slay former opponents on the very day we convert them; as did Elijah. In some ways, John's harsh message may have given him into the hands of Herodias, keeping him from continuing to minister to the many souls that sought out his message and baptism. Another interesting issue with Elijah, which may shed more light on John's disposition and why Jesus called him the greatest ever born of woman but the least in the kingdom of heaven (Matthew 11:11), is found in Elijah's comments to God about how he is the only one left in Israel who seeks God rather than Baal, to which God replies that "seven thousand in Israel have not bent their knee to Baal or kissed his image." (I Kings 14-18) At this point, Elijah's ministry ends and Elisha's begins. John's ministry ends at the hands of Herodias and Jesus' begins.

John's ministry sets the stage for Jesus'. In a dramatic speech to the Sadducees who come out to him to be baptized, John foreshadows the one who is coming in Matthew 3:10-12: "Even now the ax lies at the root of the trees. Therefore, every tree that doesn't bring forth good fruit is cut down, and cast into the fire. I indeed baptize you in water for repentance, but he who comes after me is mightier than I, whose shoes I am not worthy to carry. He will baptize you in the Holy Spirit. His winnowing fork is in his hand, and he will thoroughly cleanse his threshing floor. He will gather his wheat into the barn, but the chaff he will burn up with unquenchable fire." John explains that he had been told by the Lord that he would know the Messiah by a sign. This is in John 1:30-36: "The next day, he [John] saw Jesus coming to him, and said, 'Behold, the Lamb of God, who takes away the sin of the world! This is he of whom I said, "After me comes a man who is preferred before me, for he was before me." I didn't know him, but for this reason I came baptizing in water: that he would be revealed to Israel.' John testified, saying, 'I have seen the Spirit descending like a dove out of heaven, and it remained on him. I didn't recognize him, but he who sent me to baptize in water, he said to me, "On whomever you will see the Spirit descending, and remaining on him, the same is he who baptizes in the Holy Spirit." I have seen, and have testified that this is the Son of God.'"

As powerful as this passage is, it does have one peculiar element: John says that "he didn't know him" and that he "didn't recognize him." Since we know John and Jesus' mothers were cousins and had their sons at about the same time and that these two boys went into Egypt together, what is John saying? Perhaps the answer is that Jesus, for all his divinity, appeared perfectly normal and human on the outside. Therefore, John did know Jesus the man but did not recognize that he was the Son of God incarnate until later, until God revealed it to him.

JESUS' MINISTRY

After Egypt, Jesus, now a man, returned to the Holy Lands. He found John baptizing along the Jordan River and asked John to baptize him. John replied, "I need to be baptized by you, and you come to me?" But Jesus, revealing his own sense of humility and propriety, requested that John "allow it now, for this is the fitting way for us to fulfill all righteousness." Thus John baptized Jesus. When Jesus came up out of the water, the Gospels record that "the heavens were opened to him. He saw the Spirit of God descending as a dove, and coming on him." He, and apparently those around him, also heard a voice out of the heavens saying, "This is my beloved Son, with whom I am well pleased." After this momentous event it must have been surprising that the Spirit of God led him out into the desert to be tempted by the devil, as recorded in the Gospels.

A Broader View

In the desert Jesus fasted for forty days. When hunger became acute, he sought something to eat. At that moment the tempter appeared and delivered the first of three tests: "If you are the Son of God, command that these stones become bread." Jesus, his human side in real need of bread, took hold of a higher perspective from a time long ago when the people were sorely hungry and God fed them with manna from heaven, recalling a quote from Deuteronomy 8:3: "It is written, 'Man shall not live by bread alone, but by every word that proceeds out of the mouth of God.'" Gratifying of physical needs and wants takes a lower priority than maintaining the right perspective on one's relationship to, and trust in, God. But the devil can quote scripture, too, so he took Jesus to the Holy City and sat him on the pinnacle of the great Temple (presumably this occurred in spirit). Then the tempter challenged him: "If you are the Son of God, throw yourself down, for it is written, 'He will give his angels charge concerning you.' And, 'On their hands they will bear you up, so that you don't dash your foot against a stone.'" Both are quotes from Psalm 91:11. To this temptation Jesus countered, "Again, it is written, 'You shall not test the Lord, your God,'" which is a quote from Deuteronomy 6:16: "You shall not put the Lord your God to the test." Here Jesus affirms faith and patience, trusting God and the promises, no matter how seemingly impossible they appear to be, rather than demanding signs and proofs from God. Finally, the devil took Jesus to an exceedingly high mountain and showed him "all the kingdoms of the world and their glory." The tempter said to him, "I will give you all of these things, if you will fall down and worship me." To this temptation Jesus gave his strongest response, a command: "Get behind me, Satan! For it is written, 'You shall worship the Lord your God, and him only shall you serve.'" Which is another quote from Deuteronomy, 6:13-14: "You shall fear [reverence] the Lord your God; and him shall you serve, and shall swear by his name. You shall not go after other gods, of the gods of the peoples who are round about you." This reply affirms one of the most important principles of modern faiths: One God. And it gives a singleness of mind and action that is so important to fully realizing the spiritualization process in human life.

After this, the tempter leaves Jesus, and the Gospels tell us that angels came and ministered to his needs. When one's priorities are in the right order, all the powers of heaven engage in our lives.

At this point in Jesus' readiness to begin his ministry, his fellow teacher and baptizer, John, is arrested and put into prison by Herod Antipas. Jesus then withdrew into the region of Galilee. After visiting Nazareth, his childhood town, he lived in Capernaum, which is by the Sea of Galilee, in the region of Zebulun and Naphtali. The Gospels say that this fulfilled Isaiah's prophecy: "The land of Zebulun and the land of Naphtali, toward the sea, beyond the Jordan, Galilee of the Gentiles, the people who sat in darkness saw a great light, to those who sat in the region and shadow of death, to them light has dawned." (Isaiah 9:1-2)

The Gospels record that in this region Jesus began to preach, saying, "Repent! For the Kingdom of Heaven is at hand." Around the Sea of Galilee he began to gather his disciples, telling the fishermen brothers, Peter and Andrew, "Come with me and I will make you fishers for men." Initially, he gathered around himself twelve disciples. The Gospel of Matthew identifies them: "The first, Simon, who is called Peter; Andrew, his brother; James the son of Zebedee; John, his brother; Philip; Bartholomew [or, Nathanael, in John 1:42]; Thomas; Matthew the tax collector [publican]; James the son of Alphaeus; and Lebbaeus, whose surname was Thaddaeus [or, Judas, in Jude 1]; Simon the Canaanite; and Judas Iscariot, who also betrayed him."

Jesus gave these twelve "authority over unclean spirits, to cast them out, and to heal every disease and every sickness." The twelve are referred to as "apostles," from the Greek *apostello*, which means "to send forth" or "to dispatch," which is exactly what Jesus does. Matthew records their directive from Jesus as follows (Matthew 10): Jesus sent these twelve out, and charged them, saying, "Don't go among the Gentiles, and don't enter into any city of the Samaritans. Rather, go to the lost sheep of the house of Israel. As you go, preach, saying, 'The Kingdom of Heaven is at hand!' Heal the sick, cleanse the lepers, and cast out demons. Freely you received, so freely give. Don't take any gold, nor silver, nor brass in your money belts. Take no bag for your journey, neither two coats, nor shoes, nor staff: for the laborer is worthy of his food. Into whatever city or village you enter, find out who in it is worthy; and stay there until you go on. As you enter into the household, greet it. If the household is worthy, let your peace come on it, but if it isn't worthy, let your peace return to you. Whoever doesn't receive you, nor hear your words, as you go out of that house or that city, shake off the dust from your feet. Most assuredly I tell you, it will be more tolerable for the land of Sodom and Gomorrah in the day of judgment than for that city."

Then he warned them: "Behold, I send you out as sheep in the midst of wolves. Therefore be wise as serpents, and harmless as doves. But beware of men: for they will deliver you up to councils, and in their synagogues they will scourge you. Yes, and you will be brought before governors and kings for my sake, for a testimony to them and to the Gentiles. But when they deliver you up, don't be anxious about how or what you will say, for it will be given you in that hour what you will say. For it is not you who speak, but the Spirit of your Father who speaks in you."

He then describes what the circumstances are: "Brother will deliver up brother to death, and the father his child. Children will rise up against parents, and cause them to be put to death. You will be hated by all men for my name's sake, but he who endures to the end will be saved. But when they persecute you in this city, flee into the next, for most assuredly I tell you, you will not have gone through the cities of Israel, until the Son of Man has come. A disciple is not above his teacher, nor a servant above his lord. It is enough for the disciple that he be like his teacher, and the servant like his lord. If they have called the master of the house Beelzebul, how much more those of his household! Therefore don't be afraid of them, for there is nothing covered that will not be revealed; and hidden that will not be known. What I tell you in the darkness, speak in the light; and what you hear whispered in the ear, proclaim on the housetops."

Then he comforts and encourages them saying, "Don't be afraid of those who kill the body, but are not able to kill the soul. Rather, fear him who is able to destroy both soul and body in Gehenna (Hell). Aren't two sparrows sold for an assarion? Not one of them falls on the ground apart from your Father's will, but the very hairs of your head are all numbered. Therefore don't be afraid. You are of more value than many sparrows. Everyone therefore who confesses me before men, him I will also confess before my Father who is in heaven. But whoever denies me before men, him I will also deny before my Father who is in heaven."

Now he touches on a defining issue. Is Jesus a prophet of peace and happiness, of prosperity and comfort? Or is he a prophet of change, of a struggle that calls all humans to reach new heights of faith, consciousness, spirituality, and love? "Don't think that I came to send peace on the earth. I didn't come to send peace, but a sword. For I came to set a man at odds against his father, and a daughter against her mother, and a daughter-in-law against her mother-in-law. A man's foes will be those of his own household. He who loves father or mother more than me [the Spirit of God speaking through him] is not worthy of me; and he who loves son or daughter more than me isn't worthy of me. He who doesn't take up his cross and follow after me, isn't worthy of me. He who finds his life will lose it; and he who loses his life for my sake will find it. He who receives you receives me, and he who receives me receives him who sent me. He who receives a prophet in the name of a prophet will receive a prophet's reward: and he who receives a righteous man in the name of a righteous man will receive a righteous man's reward. Whoever gives one of these little ones just a cup of cold water to drink in the name of a disciple, most assuredly I tell you he will in no way lose his reward."

Jesus' message was a message for those who were not satisfied, who were hoping, longing, seeking a better way, and not just a better material life but a more enlightening spiritual life. He reveals these in his famous beatitudes: "Blessed are the poor in spirit, for theirs is the Kingdom of Heaven. Blessed are those who mourn, for they shall be comforted. Blessed are the meek, for they shall inherit the earth. Blessed are those who hunger and thirst after righteousness, for they shall be filled. Blessed are the merciful, for they shall obtain mercy. Blessed are the pure in heart, for they shall see God. Blessed are the peacemakers, for they shall be called children of God. Blessed are those who have been persecuted for righteousness' sake, for theirs is the Kingdom of Heaven. Blessed are you when people reproach you, persecute you, and say all kinds of evil against you falsely, for my sake. Rejoice, and be exceedingly glad, for great is your reward in heaven. For that is how they persecuted the prophets who were before you."

A Broader View

One of the greatest indications of Jesus' values is revealed to us when the imprisoned John the Baptist sends two of his disciples to ask Jesus if he is indeed the hoped for Messiah. One has to wonder how John could ask such a question, after seeing the signs of Jesus' calling in Egypt and again during and after baptizing him. It goes to show just how difficult it is for our human side to keep hold of the spiritual blessings and signs we have received, especially when the physical presses hard against us, as it was for John. Jesus chooses to answer John's inquiry by listing the activities that reflect the presence of God's Spirit. They are not the mighty things that impress men but the quiet, personal, loving things that reveal the true nature of our Maker and His relationship with us: "Go and tell John the things which you hear and see: the blind receive their sight, the lame walk, the lepers are cleansed, the deaf hear, the dead are raised up, and the poor have good news preached to them. Blessed is he who finds no occasion for stumbling in me."

In a prayer conversation with God, Jesus provides us with more insight into his views and mission and the nature of God's way: "I thank you, Father, Lord of heaven and earth, that you hid these things from the wise and understanding, and revealed them to infants. Yes, Father, for so it was well-pleasing in your sight. All things have been delivered to me by my Father. No one knows the Son, except the Father; neither does anyone know the Father, except the Son, and he to whom the Son desires to reveal him. Come to me, all you who labor and are heavily burdened, and I will give you rest. Take my yoke upon you, and learn from me, for I am gentle and lowly in heart; and you will find rest for your souls. For my yoke is easy, and my burden is light."

Jesus went around doing good, preaching goodness and the need to prepare for the kingdom of heaven. He taught in the countryside, in the synagogues, at social occasions, and in debates with the authorities. He taught individuals and small groups privately as well as publicly.

THE PASSION

As we learned in the previous chapter, these were dangerous times politically; many forces were competing for power and their way of life. It was inevitable if not destined, that Jesus would be seen as a threat to some group and attacked. His arrest, trial, persecution and execution were swift, occurring within a matter of two days! The capital charge against him was blasphemy. His many statements and claims to be personally connected with God and of God and even a God could not be tolerated and were punishable by death. The evidence against Jesus was his own words. When Jesus spoke of God he used the Hebrew word *Abba*, which means Father or Papa. In the mind of those present, no one was that personally related to God. Jesus also called himself "the son of God," explaining that even the Scriptures say that we are all gods, sons and daughters of the Most High (Psalm 82:6). What was most damning was that Jesus had delivered one of his key presentations on this issue in the Temple before the scribes, Pharisees, and members of the Sanhedrin. At this event the people present became so upset that they took up stones to stone Jesus. The account of this event is in the Gospel of John, Chapter 10: "They took up stones to stone him. Jesus answered them, 'I have shown you many good works from my Father. For which of those works do you stone me?' They answered him, 'We don't stone you for a good work, but for blasphemy, because you, being a man, make yourself God.'" This was their number one reason for crucifying him. In their minds and in the minds of many today, no man or woman could be a son or daughter of God in the truest sense of these words – godlings of God. That was so horrendous a statement that it was the worst kind of blasphemy. Jesus made a second attempt to get this teaching across to the stone throwers; he asked them: "Isn't it written in your law, 'I said, you are gods?' If he called them gods, to whom the word of God came, and the Scripture cannot be broken, do you say of him whom the Father sanctified and sent into the world, 'You blaspheme,' because I said, 'I am the Son of God?'" (John 10:34-36). The scripture to which Jesus is referring is Psalm 82, verse 6, which states: "I said, 'You are gods, All of you are sons of the Most High.'" It is not clear who is speaking in the first person in this psalm, but it was written by Asaph, a prominent psalmist in David's court. One could assume that it is "the Spirit of the Lord" that came upon so many of the Old Testament prophets and teachers. Psalm 82 begins with a line indicating that there is a large contingent of gods under God's authority: "God presides in the great assembly. He judges among the gods." This psalm, and Jesus' support of it, plainly states that we are indeed gods within a great assembly of gods that the Most High God presides over and judges. We are the sons and daughters of God. We were initially made in the image of God, later made of the dust of the Earth.

For many reasons, some political, Jesus was found guilty and sentenced to death. But not before the Romans scourged him severely. Mel Gibson's new movie, *The Passion of the Christ*, is criticized for showing this event too graphically, but in truth it was very likely as Gibson's movie portrays it. Flogging was a legal Roman practice before any execution. Only women and Roman senators or soldiers (except in cases of desertion) were exempt. A short whip (*flagellum*) was used. It was made of several braided leather thongs of varying lengths, and in these thongs small iron balls or sharp pieces of sheep bones were tied at intervals. The condemned man was stripped of his clothing, his hands tied to an upright post, and his back, buttocks, and legs were flogged either by two soldiers (*lictors*) or by one who alternated positions. The scourging was intended to weaken the victim to a state just short of collapse or death. As the soldiers repeatedly struck the victim's back with full force, the iron balls would cause deep contusions, and the leather thongs and sheep bones would cut into the skin and subcutaneous tissues. Then, as the flogging continued, the lacerations would tear into the underlying skeletal muscles. Strips of bleeding flesh would be opened. Pain and blood loss generally set the stage for circulatory shock. The extent of blood loss probably determined how long the victim survived on the cross. Outside the Praetorium, the governor's residence in Jerusalem, Jesus was severely whipped. The customary number of lashes was 39, in accordance with Jewish law. But the Gospels indicate that the Roman soldiers were scornful of him because of the charge against him and his claims of godliness and kingship, and likely took out their feelings in an unusually severe whipping. After the scourging, the soldiers were amused by the sight of this bleeding man who had claimed to be a king, and they began to mock him by placing a robe on his shoulders, a crown of thorns on his head, and a wooden staff as a scepter in his right hand. According to the account in Matthew 27:27, this was done before the whole battalion, which would have been about 500 soldiers! They mocked him by kneeling before him and saying, "Hail, King of the Jews!" They then spat on him and struck him on the head with the wooden staff, asking him to reveal who hit him. The severe scourging, with its intense pain, blood loss, and torn skin would render his body particularly tender and weak. The physical and mental abuse meted out by the crowds and soldiers, along with the lack of food, water, and sleep, would have contributed to his weakened physical condition and inability to carry his cross up the hill. Therefore, even before the actual crucifixion, Jesus' physical state was likely critical. The procession from the Praetorium to

Golgotha ("place of the skulls") is believed to have included Jesus, two other prisoners (thieves), a centurion (commander of 100 soldiers), and a few soldiers assigned to this execution. As we are told in the Gospels, Jesus could not carry his cross the whole way, as apparently the other two prisoners were able to do. This indicates that his beating had been worse than the others'. Simon of Cyrene, who was just coming into the city from the countryside, was compelled by the soldiers to carry the cross for Jesus. Simon and his sons, Alexander and Rufus, must have been known to the Gospel writers; perhaps he or his sons were followers of Jesus. Rufus is mentioned in Romans 16:13. As the cross was being shifted from Jesus to Simon, Jesus was offered wine with myrrh, which was considered then to be a sedative. But Jesus refused to drink it.

Once they reached Golgotha, the prisoners would have been stripped of most of their garments before being put on their respective crosses. The Roman governor had commanded his soldiers to put a sign on Jesus' cross that read, "The King of the Jews." People walking by derided Jesus, yelling, "Aha! You who would destroy the Temple and build it in three days, save yourself, and come down from that cross!" The chief priests were present, and they said, "He saved others; he cannot save himself. Let the Christ, the King of Israel, come down now from the cross, that we may see and believe."

The piercing of Jesus' hands and feet would have caused his remaining bodily fluids to drain. It's little wonder that he died within hours of being hung on the cross. The Gospels indicate that the crucifixion began at about nine in the morning (the "third hour"). Around noon (the "sixth hour") the sky became dark. Around three o'clock (the "ninth hour") Jesus cried out in a loud voice: "Eli, Eli, lama sabach-thani?" Which is interpreted in the Gospels as: "My God, My God, why have you forsaken me?" Now it had been dark since noon, and this cry caused bystanders to become alarmed. Some of them cried out that Jesus was calling Elijah. One got a sponge, soaked it in vinegar, put it on a long reed, and extended it up to Jesus' mouth to drink. But another stopped him, saying, "Wait, let us see whether Elijah will come to take him down."

Present throughout these hours of suffering were the many Holy Women who traveled with Jesus: Mary, his mother; Mary, the mother of James; Elois, the mother of the sons of Zebedee, James and John; Mary Magdalene; Salome, who ministered to Jesus in Galilee; and many other women who came up with Jesus to Jerusalem. In addition, some of his disciples were present, most notably John, to whom Jesus assigned the care of his mother.

Following the cry for Elijah, if that is what it was, Jesus let out a loud cry and breathed his last breath. The Gospel of Luke, 23:46, gives us the words of this loud cry: "Father, into your hands I commend my spirit!" This cry is also found in Psalm 31:5: "Into your hand I commend my spirit. You redeem me, Lord, God of truth."

At the moment of his death, the curtain in the Temple that separated the people from the Holy of Holies tore in two, from top to bottom – signifying that the veil between humanity's consciousness and God's had been opened. The stain of original sin that had blocked full communion between humanity and our Creator was cleansed. The way was now open.

The centurion who stood facing Jesus as he breathed his last breath, and had seen many men die, said, "Truly this man was a Son of God!"

When evening came, Joseph, a rich man from Arimathea, who was a disciple of Christ, went to Pilate and asked for the body of Jesus. Pilate ordered that it be given to Joseph, which upset the Sanhedrin leaders, because they knew of the prophecy that he would rise from death. They implored Pilate to put a guard on Jesus' tomb so that there would be no way that Jesus' followers could claim that he rose from death. Pilate agreed, and the tomb was put under Roman guard. However, some texts indicate that the guards were not Roman but of the Sanhedrin soldiery. This would explain why Matthew's Gospel has the tomb guards reporting to the chief priests rather than Pilate.

RESURRECTION

Friday night Jesus' body was laid to rest. The next day, Saturday, was the sabbath of the Jews. The guards would have been on duty all day. The following day was considered to be the first day of the new week, the week beginning on Sunday. Around dawn of this day, Mary Magdalene, Joanna, and the "other Mary," mother of James, Joseph (sometimes called *Joses*), and Salome, came to the tomb to complete the rites of burial. In Mark's account of these events, the women were talking amongst themselves, concerned about moving the huge stone that had been placed over the entrance to the tomb. These stones were like huge wheels that rolled in a gutter to close a tomb. Tombs were usually carved in rock, with several niches to receive bodies. When the women arrived, to their astonishment, the stone was rolled away from the entrance. Upon entering the tomb, they saw a "young man" dressed in a white robe, sitting on the right side. He said to them, "Do not be amazed; you seek Jesus of Nazareth, who was crucified. He has risen, he is not here; see the place where they laid him. But go, tell his disciples and Peter that he is going before you to Galilee; there you will see him, as he told you." The women, trembling, astonished, and filled with joy, ran from the tomb and told no one along their way, because they were afraid. The young man in the white robe may have named Peter specifically to ease Peter's pain over his denying that he knew Jesus during the trial on Thursday night. In Matthew's account of these events, an angel of the Lord descended from heaven as the women approached the tomb, caused an earthquake to roll back the huge stone, and gave the women the message. In this account, the guards also saw and heard the angel and reported it to the chief priests. In this account, Jesus appears to the women before they actually reach the disciples, and tells them, "Do not be afraid; go and tell my brethren to go to Galilee, and there they will see me." Eventually, the women reached the disciples, including Peter, and gave them the message. All the Gospels record that the male disciples did not believe the women.

During this same dawn, Jesus appeared to two of his disciples on the road to a village called Emmaus, about seven miles from Jerusalem. The two disciples were talking about all of the events that had occurred and their meaning. Jesus, apparently walking as any normal man, approached them and walked with them. He asked, "What is this conversation which you are holding with each other as you walk?" They stopped and, looking sad, asked him, "Are you the only visitor to Jerusalem who does not know the things that have happened there in these days?" Jesus replied, "What things?" They told him: "The things concerning Jesus, the Nazarene, who was a prophet mighty in deed and word before God and all the people; and how the chief priests and our rulers delivered him up to be condemned to death, and crucified him. But we were hoping that it was he who would redeem Israel. Yes, and besides all this, it is now the third day since these things happened. Also, certain women of our company amazed us, having arrived early at the tomb; and when they didn't find his body, they came saying that they had also seen a vision of angels, who said that he was alive. Some of us went to the tomb, and found it just like the women had said, but they didn't see him." Jesus replied, "Foolish men, and slow of heart to believe in all that the prophets have spoken! Didn't the Christ have to suffer these things and to enter into his glory?" Then Jesus explained all of the

Scriptures to them, beginning with Moses and all the prophets, and all the things concerning the Christ, the Messiah. When they drew near to the village, Jesus acted like he would go further on the road but hey urged him, saying, "Stay with us, for it is almost evening, and the day is almost over." He went with them, and as they sat together at the table, Jesus took the bread, gave thanks, broke it and gave it to them. The Gospel records that "their eyes were opened, and they recognized him, and he vanished out of their sight." They said one to another, "Weren't our hearts burning within us while he spoke to us along the way, and while he opened the Scriptures to us?" They rose up that very hour and returned to Jerusalem, found the eleven gathered together, and those who were with them, and told them: "The Lord is risen indeed, and has appeared to Simon!" It must be assumed that they are referring to Simon Peter, but wouldn't he be among the eleven? Whatever the case, the Scriptures do not record Simon's experience with Jesus.

These two unidentified disciples from Emmaus, obviously not among the eleven, then related the things that happened along the way and how he was recognized by them in the breaking of the bread. As they were speaking, Jesus himself appeared in their midst, and said to them, "Peace be to you." The Gospels record that they were terrified and filled with fear and assumed that they were seeing a spirit. But Jesus said, "Why are you troubled? Why do doubts arise in your hearts? See my hands and my feet, that it is truly me. Touch me and see, for a spirit doesn't have flesh and bones, as you see that I have." When he had said this, he showed them his hands and his feet. While they still didn't believe for joy, and wondered, he said to them, "Do you have anything here to eat?" This must have been an astonishing request, but the disciples gave him a piece of a broiled fish and some honey in the honeycomb, which he ate in front of them. He said to them, "This is what I told you, while I was still with you, that all things which are written in the law of Moses, the prophets, and the psalms, concerning me must be fulfilled." Then he opened their minds, that they might understand the Scriptures. He said to them, "Thus it is written, and thus it was necessary for the Christ to suffer and to rise from the dead the third day, and that repentance and remission of sins should be preached in his name to all the nations, beginning at Jerusalem. You are witnesses of these things. Behold, I send forth the promise of my Father on you. But wait in the city of Jerusalem until you are clothed with power from on high." The Gospels record that he then led them out as far as Bethany, lifted up his hands, and blessed them. During his blessing he was carried up into heaven and disappeared from them. The Gospels record that they worshiped him and returned to Jerusalem with great joy and were continually in the Temple, praising and blessing God.

In I Corinthians 15:3-8, Paul lists the appearances of the risen Christ: "He was raised on the third day according to the Scriptures, and appeared to Cephas [Simon Peter], then to the twelve. Then he appeared to over five hundred brothers at once, most of whom remain until now, but some have also fallen asleep [passed on]. Then he appeared to James, then to all the apostles, and last of all, as to the child born at the wrong time, he appeared to me also." Paul seems to overlook that Jesus first appeared to the holy women. His own experience with the risen Jesus came while he was under the authority of the Sanhedrin to arrest all who were a part of "The Way," the first name used for the followers of Jesus. Acts 9:3 begins with the description of Saul's conversion to Paul, after Jesus had appeared to him:

"Saul, still breathing threats and slaughter against the disciples of the Lord, went to the high priest, and asked for letters from him to the synagogues of Damascus, that if he found any who were of the Way, whether men or women, he might bring them bound to Jerusalem. As he traveled, it happened that he got close to Damascus, and suddenly a light from the sky shone around him. He fell on the earth, and heard a voice saying to him, 'Saul, Saul, why do you persecute me?' He said, 'Who are you, Lord?' The Lord said, 'I am Jesus, whom you are persecuting. But rise up, and enter into the city, and you will be told what you must do.' The men who traveled with him stood speechless, hearing the sound, but seeing no one. Saul arose from the ground, and when his eyes were opened, he saw no one. They led him by the hand, and brought him into Damascus. He was without sight for three days, and neither ate nor drank."

Notice that Jesus' appearance to Saul was more like a powerful light-being from the sky than in his resurrected physical body. This type of appearance continues when Jesus again appears to a disciple in Damascus, named Ananias. Jesus appears, calls out, "Ananias!" to which he replies, "Behold, it's me, Lord." Acts records the event as follows:

> The Lord said to him, "Arise, and go to the street which is called Straight, and inquire in the house of Judas for one named Saul, a man of Tarsus. For behold, he is praying, and in a vision he has seen a man named Ananias coming in, and laying his hands on him, that he might receive his sight." But Ananias answered, "Lord, I have heard from many about this man, how much evil he did to your saints at Jerusalem. Here he has authority from the chief priests to bind all who call on your name." But the Lord said to him, "Go your way, for he is my chosen vessel to bear my name before the nations and kings, and the children of Israel. For I will show him how many things he must suffer for my name's sake." Ananias departed, and entered into the

house. Laying his hands on him, he said, "Brother Saul, the Lord, who appeared to you on the road by which you came, has sent me, that you may receive your sight, and be filled with the Holy Spirit." Immediately something like scales fell from his eyes, and he received his sight. He arose and was baptized. He took food and was strengthened. Saul stayed several days with the disciples who were at Damascus. Immediately in the synagogues he proclaimed the Christ, that he is the Son of God. All who heard him were amazed, and said, "Isn't this he who in Jerusalem made havoc of those who called on this name? And he had come here intending to bring them bound before the chief priests!" But Saul increased more in strength, and confounded the Jews who lived at Damascus, proving that this is the Christ. When many days were fulfilled, the Jews conspired together to kill him, but their plot became known to Saul. They watched the gates both day and night that they might kill him, but his disciples took him by night, and let him down through the wall, lowering him in a basket. When Saul had come to Jerusalem, he tried to join himself to the disciples; but they were all afraid of him, not believing that he was a disciple.

THE ASCENSION AND THE HOLY SPIRIT

This phenomenon of Christ appearing, instructing, and guiding incarnate people while remaining in heaven was first explained by Jesus at the Last Supper discussion, as recorded in John 14 through 16. In John 14:16-17 Jesus explains: "I will pray to the Father, and he will give you another Counselor, that he may be with you forever – the Spirit of truth, whom the world cannot receive; for it doesn't see him, neither knows him. You know him, for he lives with you, and will be in you." In John 14:26, Jesus picks up on this concept again, saying: "The Counselor, the Holy Spirit, whom the Father will send in my name, he will teach you all things, and will remind you of all that I said to you." In John 15:26, again Jesus explains about this inner Counselor: "When the Counselor has come, whom I will send to you from the Father, the Spirit of truth, who proceeds from the Father, he will testify about me." In John 16:7, he explains that he must go in order for the Spirit of Truth, the Counselor to come: "Nevertheless I tell you the truth: It is to your advantage that I go away, for if I don't go away, the Counselor won't come to you. But if I go, I will send him to you." Finally, in John 16:12-13, Jesus gives us all the means to learn more from the inner guidance of the Spirit of Truth: "I have yet many things to tell you, but you can't bear them now. However when he, the Spirit of truth, has come, he will guide you into all truth, for he will not speak from himself; but whatever he hears, he will speak. He will declare to you things that are coming."

We see the Holy Spirit in action in The Acts of the Apostles, a book believed to have been by Luke or Luke's journals being used by someone else, such as Lucius, the Bishop of the Church of Laodicea in Asia Minor. Acts begins with a clear reference to the "first book," which would have been the Gospel of Luke: "The first book I wrote, Theophilus [this name literally means "lover of God," and could therefore be addressing anyone who loves God], concerned all that Jesus began both to do and to teach, until the day in which he was received up, after he had given commandment through the Holy Spirit to the apostles whom he had chosen." Notice this phrasing, "through the Holy Spirit to the apostles." Clearly Luke is conveying the understanding that the Holy Spirit is the means for continuing guidance and instruction. Luke continues: "To these he also showed himself alive after he suffered, by many proofs, appearing to them over a period of forty days, and speaking about God's Kingdom. Being assembled together with them, he charged them, 'Don't depart from Jerusalem, but wait for the promise of the Father, which you heard from me. For John indeed baptized in water, but you will be baptized in the Holy Spirit not many days from now.'"

After Jesus had given them this directive, the disciples questioned Jesus and then, Luke records, the ascension occurred. It is the same ascension that was described earlier in the Gospel of Luke, 24:50-51. Luke records it in Acts this way: "They asked him, 'Lord, are you now restoring the kingdom to Israel?' He said to them, 'It isn't for you to know times or seasons which the Father has set within His own authority. But you will receive power when the Holy Spirit has come upon you. You will be witnesses to me in Jerusalem, in all Judea and Samaria, and to the uttermost parts of the earth.' When he had said these things, as they were looking, he was taken up, and a cloud received him out of their sight. While they were looking steadfastly into the sky as he went, behold, two men stood by them in white clothing, who also said, 'You men of Galilee, why do you stand looking into the sky? This Jesus, who was received up from you into the sky will come back in the same way as you saw him going into the sky.'"

Then they returned to Jerusalem and went up into "the upper room" of the place they were staying. Luke lists those present: Peter, John, James, Andrew, Philip, Thomas, Bartholomew, Matthew, James the son of Alphaeus, Simon the Zealot, and Judas the son of James. Luke tells us, "All these with one accord continued steadfastly in prayer and supplication, along with the women, and Mary the mother of Jesus, and with his brothers." Jesus' brothers were James and Jude. His sister was Ruth. At a later meeting, Luke states that there were about 120 disciples present. It was at this meeting that Matthias was elected by lots to replace Judas Iscariot as a member of the twelve.

Seven Sabbaths after Passover, after the weekend of Jesus' death and resurrection plus one more day (making it Sunday), the Jews practiced a festival called *Shabuoth*, given to them from God through Moses (Leviticus 23:15), in which they offered, among other things, "one male goat for a sin offering, and two male lambs a year old for a sacrifice of peace offerings." Because this is fifty days after Passover (7 weeks plus one day), it is referred to by Christians as Pentecost (meaning, "fiftieth day"). This was the day on which the Holy Spirit came upon the disciples. Luke describes it:

> Now when the day of Pentecost had come, they were all with one accord in one place. Suddenly there came from the sky a sound like the rushing of a mighty wind, and it filled all the house where they were sitting. Tongues like fire appeared and were distributed to them, and one sat on each of them. They were all filled with the Holy Spirit, and began to speak with other languages, as the Spirit gave them the ability to speak. Now there were dwelling in Jerusalem Jews, devout men, from every nation under the sky. When this sound was heard, the multitude came together, and were bewildered, because everyone heard them speaking in his own language. They were all amazed and marveled, saying to one another, "Behold, aren't all these who speak Galileans? How do we hear, everyone in our own native language? Parthians, Medes, Elamites, and people from Mesopotamia, Judea, Cappadocia, Pontus, Asia, Phrygia, Pamphylia, Egypt, the parts of Libya around Cyrene, visitors from Rome, both Jews and proselytes, Cretans and Arabians; we hear them speaking in our languages the mighty works of

A Broader View

God!" They were all amazed, and were perplexed, saying one to another, "What does this mean?" Others, mocking, said, "They are filled with new wine." But Peter, standing up with the eleven, lifted up his voice, and spoke out to them, "You men of Judea, and all you who dwell at Jerusalem, let this be known to you, and listen to my words. For these aren't drunken, as you suppose, seeing it is only the third hour of the day. But this is what has been spoken through the prophet Joel: 'It will be in the last days, says God, That I will pour out my Spirit on all flesh. Your sons and your daughters will prophesy. Your young men will see visions. Your old men will dream dreams. Yes, and on my servants and on my handmaidens in those days, I will pour out my Spirit, and they will prophesy. I will show wonders in the sky above, And signs on the earth beneath; Blood, and fire, and billows of smoke. The sun will be turned into darkness, And the moon into blood, Before the great and glorious day of the Lord comes. It will be, that whoever will call on the name of the Lord will be saved.' Men of Israel, hear these words! Jesus of Nazareth, a man approved by God to you by mighty works and wonders and signs which God did by him in the midst of you, even as you yourselves know, him, being delivered up by the determined counsel and foreknowledge of God, you have taken by the hand of lawless men, crucified and killed; whom God raised up, having freed him from the agony of death, because it was not possible that he should be held by it. For David says concerning him, 'I saw the Lord always before my face, For he is on my right hand, that I should not be moved. Therefore my heart was glad, and my tongue rejoiced. Moreover my flesh also will dwell in hope; Because you will not leave my soul in Hades, Neither will you allow your Holy One to see decay. You made known to me the ways of life. You will make me full of gladness with your presence.' Brothers, I may tell you freely of the patriarch David, that he both died and was buried, and his tomb is with us to this day. Therefore, being a prophet, and knowing that God had sworn with an oath to him that of the fruit of his body, according to the flesh, he would raise up the Christ to sit on his throne, he foreseeing this spoke about the resurrection of the Christ, that neither was his soul left in Hades, nor did his flesh see decay. This Jesus God raised up, whereof we all are witnesses. Being therefore exalted by the right hand of God, and having received from the Father the promise of the Holy Spirit, he has poured out this, which you now see and hear. For David didn't ascend into the heavens, but he says himself, 'The Lord said to my Lord, "Sit by my right hand, Until I make your enemies a footstool for your feet." Let all the house of Israel therefore know assuredly that God has made him both Lord and Christ, this Jesus whom you crucified.'" Now when they heard this, they were cut to the heart, and said to Peter and the rest of the apostles, "Brothers, what shall we do?" Peter said to them, "Repent, and be baptized, everyone of you, in the name of Jesus Christ for the forgiveness of sins, and you will receive the gift of the Holy Spirit. For to you is the promise, and to your children, and to all who are far off, even as many as the Lord our God will call to himself." With many other words he testified, and exhorted them, saying, "Save yourselves from this crooked generation!" Then those who gladly received his word were baptized. There were added that day about three thousand souls. They continued steadfastly in the apostles' teaching and fellowship, in the breaking of bread, and prayer.

Luke's report clearly reveals that the Holy Spirit would come upon all who were present, from many different lands, after they accepted his testimony, were baptized, and received the forgiveness of sins given by Jesus' offering of himself to God. Three thousand joined The Way on that day. For Peter, this was truly the fulfillment of his faith in Jesus. But Peter hadn't seen anything yet. All those who joined The Way on that day and presumably received the gift of the Holy Spirit were Jews, who, to Peter, were naturally worthy of God's Spirit upon them. A short time later, after a vision from God while praying on his rooftop, Peter witnessed the Holy Spirit come upon a gathering of Gentiles – pork-eating, uncircumcised Gentiles!

Luke describes the vision that prepared Peter for this amazing event: "Peter went up on the housetop to pray at about noon. He became hungry and desired to eat, but while they were preparing, he fell into a trance. He saw heaven opened and a certain container descending to him, like a great sheet let down by four corners on the earth, in which were all kinds of four-footed animals of the earth, wild animals, reptiles, and birds of the sky. A voice came to him, 'Rise, Peter, kill and eat!' But Peter said, 'Not so, Lord; for I have never eaten anything that is common or unclean.' A voice came to him again the second time, 'What God has cleansed, you must not call unclean.' This was done three times, and immediately the vessel was received up into heaven." While Peter was attempting to understand this vision, some Gentile servants of a Roman centurion (leader of 100 men) named Cornelius yelled to him from the gate to his house, asking if he would come with them to their master's house. While hearing their plea, the Spirit said to Peter, "Behold, three men seek you. But arise, get down, and go with them, doubting nothing;

for I have sent them." Peter went down to the men and journeyed with them to the centurion's house. On the way, they explained to Peter that Cornelius had received a vision from a holy angel, directing him to invite Peter to his house and to listen to what Peter said. Cornelius was waiting for Peter with all of his relatives and dear friends. When Peter entered, Cornelius fell down at his feet and worshiped him. But Peter raised him up, saying, "Stand up! I myself am also a man." Luke describes that Peter explained to them, "You know how it is an unlawful thing for a man who is a Jew to join himself or come to one of another nation, but God has shown me that I shouldn't call any man unholy or unclean. Therefore also I came without complaint when I was sent for. I ask therefore, why did you send for me?" After Cornelius explains the vision and their readiness to hear Peter's message, Peter says, "Truly I perceive that God doesn't show favoritism; but in every nation he who fears [reverences] him and works righteousness is acceptable to him." Following this, Peter began his speech, reviewing the spiritual journey that led him and others to this new understanding. Luke then describes how the Holy Spirit came upon the Gentiles in Peter's presence: "While Peter was still speaking these words, the Holy Spirit fell on all those who heard the word. They of the circumcision who believed were amazed, as many as came with Peter, because the gift of the Holy Spirit was also poured out on the Gentiles. For they heard them speaking in other languages and magnifying God. Then Peter answered, 'Can any man forbid the water [of baptism], that these who have received the Holy Spirit as well as we should not be baptized?' He commanded them to be baptized in the name of Jesus Christ."

The Comforter, the Counselor, the Spirit of Truth, the Holy Spirit came as a result of Jesus Christ's ascension into heaven. He became an advocate for us, a bridge connecting us with our Maker, and a conduit of God's Spirit upon us.

Chapter Three
FORERUNNERS AND EARLY CHRISTIANS

The light of Christianity did not appear out of nowhere. It was not confined to a small group of people with a new message and method. On the contrary, it was the fulfillment of many generations of many peoples faithfully seeking God's presence and a greater understanding of their relationship with God. Even among the Chosen People there were many subgroups, with different experiences and approaches concerning the nature of the relationship between humans and God, the Spirit of Life and Love that gave each of us our own consciousness and life. Therefore, our journey through the rise of Christianity begins with understanding the existing people out of which much of the spirit of Christianity came. Two important groups are the Essenes and the Gnostics.

ESSENES

Most of what we know about the Essenes comes from the Dead Sea Scrolls, discovered in 1946 in caves in the hills on the western side of the Dead Sea, an area called Qumran. Additionally, Josephus, Phily, and Philo Judeaeus, all lived in that time and wrote much about the Essenes. Philo called them *Essaei*, Josephus used *Essaei* and *Esseni*; names that mean something like "holy ones." From the writings of these men we learn that the Essenes were indeed considered to be Jews by race, yet they kept themselves separate from the activities of the main body of Jews, which was comprised of Pharisees and Sadducees (Samaritans were always considered to be half-breeds, therefore not true Jews). We learn that the Essenes, though they did not believe in blood sacrifice at the Temple or in their communities, sent their offerings to the great Temple as expected but did not attend to the offerings directly themselves. They claimed that a reverent mind was the best offering to God. They did, however, live according to the Torah law.

The main virtues ascribed to the Essenes by these writers were obedience, truthfulness, continence, justice, and temperance. They had an unusual interest in helping the sick, showed great respect for the elderly, and hospitality to strangers. All men were regarded equals and slavery as being contrary to nature. The Qumran Essenes believed ethics to be the highest course of study, rejecting philosophy as useless. They were known to spend much time and effort searching for medicinal remedies in nature and devoted special care to helping the sick, no matter what their religion. They were known to possess magical powers, particularly the gift of prophecy. Josephus records that an Essene named Manahan foretold Herod the Greta's kingship when Herod was still a boy and had no outward potential for a royal position.

The Essenes held all things in common. This is confirmed by the Dead Sea Scroll titled "Community Rule," found in cave 1. Even their individual homes were considered to be the community's. They labored principally at agriculture and made farm implements or household items. Harvests and wages went to the stewards, who distributed them to each member as needed. Clothes and shoes were retained until worn out. No trading was allowed except barter. Servants were forbidden. Their leaders were elected. In towns an officer was appointed to look after traveling brethren. One hundred members constituted a court of justice whose unanimous decision was irrevocable. They were not allowed to carry weapons, except a staff for defense when traveling. This is contradicted by the scroll titled "War Scroll," found in caves 1 and 4, which clearly indicates that this community studied and prepared for war against an invading enemy called the "Kittim," or Romans. Many scholars believe the Essenes abandoned, or were driven from, Qumran when the Romans crushed the rebellion of 66-73 AD

Their daily routine was described as follows: They were up before daybreak and directed a prayer to the Sun, as if soliciting it to rise. This is perhaps their most non-Jewish practice, the source of which is unknown. After this prayer, each was sent to his appointed employment and worked until the fifth hour (eleven o'clock); then all assembled, bathed in water, and laying aside their work garments, clothed themselves in white. They then silently entered a common dining area. Each of them received bread and a dish of food. After a priest said grace, they ate together. At the end of this break a prayer was again said. They then laid aside their white garments, resuming their ordinary attire, and worked again until evening. At the evening break, they dined in the same manner.

The noonday meal was regarded as a sacrificial meal, being prepared by their priests. No stranger was admitted to this meal. Yet, at dinner, strangers were allowed. Essenes spoke only in turn and were moderate in food and drink. Essenes were not allowed to eat anything prepared by outsiders. Outsiders wrote that the silence at Essene meals created a strange and mysterious ambiance.

Many of the Essenes reached a great age, and they acquired such strength of mind and body that the worst torments inflicted on them by the Romans failed to shake them, and they met death with a smile.

Most of the Essenes did not marry. Those who did, did so specifically to create a family in order for souls to come into the community. Records reveal that they also perpetuated their sect by adopting children and admitting adults who were, according to Pliny, "wearying of battling with the rough sea of life." For an adult to join their community they had to undergo a three-year transition process. Upon arriving, the stranger received an apron to wear at their ablutions, a white garment for meals and special events, and a little spade-like instrument with which to dig a hole and cover their excrement from the rays of the sun. For one year they lived on the outskirts of the community, but adhered to the community's ascetic rules. Then, for the next two years, they shared in the purification rites, but not in the mid-day meals of the initiated. If found satisfactory, they were chosen full members and bound themselves by oath to honor God, observe justice, be loyal to all but especially to those in authority, and if ever in authority themselves, not to outshine others. They swore to love truth and honesty, to conceal nothing from their fellows while revealing nothing to strangers. They also swore to keep secret the Essene scrolls and the names of their angels. This was the only time when Essenes took oaths, their word being regarded by all as so sacred that Herod excused them from the oath of allegiance.

The Dead Sea Scrolls, found in eleven caves in the hills of Qumran, are of three types: 1. Scrolls that reproduce the Torah, 2. Scrolls that are not accepted into the canon of Jewish faith but are considered to be sacred, and 3. Scrolls related to the Essene commune, containing ordinances, biblical commentaries, apocalyptic visions, and liturgical works.

Here is an example of how the scrolls read. The ellipses denote missing text; many of the scrolls are fragmented. These words are from "The Scroll of Secrets":

This shall be the sign that this shall come to pass: when the sources of evil are shut up and wickedness is banished in the presence of righteousness, as darkness in the presence of light, or as smoke vanishes and is no more, in the same way wickedness will vanish forever and righteousness will be manifest like the sun. The world will be made firm and all the adherents of the secrets of sin shall be no more. True knowledge shall fill the world and there will never be any more folly. This is all ready to happen, it is a true oracle, and by this it shall be known to you that it cannot be averted.

It is true that all the peoples reject evil, yet it advances in all of them. It is true that truth is esteemed in the utterances of all the nations - yet is there any tongue or language that grasp it? What nation wants to be oppressed by another that is stronger? Or who wants his money to be stolen by a wicked man? Yet what nation is there that has not oppressed its neighbor? Where is the people that has not robbed?

So listen, you who hold fast to the wonderful secrets ... of eternity, and the plots behind every deed, and the purpose of .... He knows every secret and stands behind every thought. He does every ... the Lord of all is He, from long ago He established it, and forever ... the purpose of the origins he opened up to ... for he tests His son, and gives as an inheritance ... every secret, and he limits of every deed; and what ... the Gentiles, for He created them and their deeds....

Consider the soothsayers, those teachers of sin. Say the parable, declare the riddle before we speak; then you will know if you have understood. ...your foolishness, for the vision is sealed up from you, and you have not properly understood the eternal mysteries and you have not become wise in understanding ... for you have not properly understood the origin of Wisdom; but if you should unseal the vision ... all your wisdom, for to you.... Hear now what wisdom is.

...lights of the stars for a memorial of His name ... hidden things of the mysteries of Light and the ways of Darkness ... the times of heat with the periods of cold ... the breaking of day and the coming of night ... the origins of things....

How can a man understand without knowledge or hearing? ... He created insight for His children, by much wisdom He uncovered our ears that we may hear.... He created insight for all those who pursue true knowledge and ... all wisdom is from eternity; it may not be changed ... He locked up behind the waters, so that not ... the heaven above heaven....

...and He is well known for His patience, and might in His great anger, and splendid ... He in His numerous acts of mercy, and terrible in His wrathful purposes, and honored ... and over the land He made him a ruler, and God is honored among His Holy people, and splendid among His chosen, yes , splendid ... holy, great in the blessing of ... their splendor and ... when the Era of Wickedness is at an end...."

The Scroll of Secrets is considered to be one of the seven prophecy scrolls discovered in the caves at Qumran. As you can see, it reveals that there will come a time when evil is no more. It reveals that the Essenes believed that wisdom comes from within a person, asking, "How can a man understand without knowledge or hearing?" And then answering, "He [God] created insight for His children ... He uncovered our ears that we may hear ... He created insight for all those who pursue true knowledge ... all wisdom is from eternity." Notice also how wise they are about human nature, saying: "It is true that all the peoples reject evil, yet it advances in all of them. It is true that truth is esteemed in the utterances of all the nations – yet is there any tongue or language that grasp it? What nation wants to be oppressed by another that is stronger? Or who wants his money to be stolen by a wicked man? Yet what nation is there that has not oppressed its neighbor? Where is the people that has not robbed?"

Many researchers have seen in the Essenes the foundations for Christianity. And we know that many of Jesus' relatives and friends were members or friends of the Essene community. Compare the following teachings of the New Testament with those in the Essene Scrolls:

"Blessed are the meek, for they shall inherit the earth." Matt. 5:5

"But the meek shall possess the land, and delight themselves in abundant prosperity," Psalm 37:11, a psalm that the Scrolls focused much attention on, and the community considered themselves to be "the meek."

"Blessed are the poor in spirit, for theirs is the kingdom of heaven." Matt. 5:3

"Among the poor in spirit is power." War scroll, XIV, 7.

"You must therefore be perfect just as your heavenly Father is perfect." Matt. 5:8
"Who walk in the way of perfection as commanded by God." Community Rule scroll, VIII, 21.

In Matthew 21:42, Jesus refers to Isaiah 28:16 and Psalm 118:22: "Have you never read in the scriptures: 'The very stone which the builders rejected has become the head of the corner'; this was the Lord's doing, and it is marvelous in our eyes?" In the Community Rule scroll, VIII, 7, the same references are made, stating that "the Council of the Community ... shall be that tried wall, that precious corner stone."

The Christian concept of "saint" may actually find its origin in the Dead Sea Scrolls. The opening line in the Community Rule reads: "The Master shall teach the saints to live according to the Book of the Community Rule." But saints is not a concept found in other Jewish writings.

Consider also the early Christian customs and concepts concerning baptism, communal ownership, twelve apostles (three of whom held a special place in Jesus' activities: Peter, James, and John, who were the only ones allowed to be present at the raising of Jairus' daughter and the Transfiguration), and acceptance of a Messiah among us. The Community Rule scroll addresses all of these:

Baptism, begun by John the Baptist, an Essene himself, was a ritual among the Essenes. In Community Rule, III, 7, it states that the new member "shall be cleansed from all his sins by the spirit of holiness uniting him to truth ... and when his flesh is sprinkled with purifying water and sanctified by cleansing water, it shall be made clean by the humble submission of his soul to all the precepts of God." That is clearly the sacrament of Baptism.

In Acts 2:44-46, the members of the early Christian Church held all things in common: "All who believed were together and had all things in common; and they sold their possessions and goods and distributed them to all, as any had need. And day by day, attending the temple together [the Temple was not destroyed until 70 AD] and breaking bread in their homes, they partook of food with glad and generous hearts." In the Community Rule scroll we have these passages: "All ... shall bring all their knowledge, powers, and possessions into the Community. They shall eat in common and pray in common."

Christianity, from as early as the Acts of the Apostles, holds that there were twelve apostles, three of whom had a special role. Galatians actually identifies the initial authorities of the fledgling church to have been James, the brother of Jesus; Peter; and John. Fascinatingly, the Community Rule scroll indicates that the Qumran community was governed by a council of twelve individuals, with three priests having special roles.

Among the Jewish sects of the time, the Essenes were the most avid believers in a Messiah. To everyone's amazement, the War Scroll contains a six-line fragment that describes the Messiah as a "Pierced Messiah," a reference that so reflects what happened to Jesus on the cross that it created a great stir of interest when first publicized in *Time* magazine, September 1992. The scrolls' references to a "wounded" and "pierced" Messiah, combined with references to the role of the High Priest as chief among those convincing the Romans and the people to crucify Jesus, have caused many to believe that this passage foresees the manner of Jesus' death, and that that death was the prophesied death of the Messiah. The fragment is referred to as 4Q285, and reads as follows:
"Isaiah the prophet: The thickets of the forest will be cut down with an axe and Lebanon by a majestic one will fall. And there shall come forth a shoot from the stump of Jesse ... the Branch of David and they will enter into judgment with ... and they killed the Prince of the Congregation, the Branch of David ... by strokes [scourging] and by wounds [piercings]. And a Priest of renown [High Priest] will command ... the slain of the Kittim [i.e. Romans]."

The Messiah prophesied in Daniel by the angel Gabriel is a wounded Messiah. In reading Gabriel's prophecy we have to first understand that Daniel is in captivity in Babylon when the angel gives the prophecy; the Temple and Jerusalem have been destroyed by the Babylonians. The first rebuilding spoken of in the prophecy is conducted many years later with the participation of Jesse, mentioned in the War Scroll. Then building begins again during Herod the Great's reign and the coming of Jesus. Here is Gabriel's prophecy as recorded in Daniel 9:25-27:

> Know therefore and discern, that from the going forth of the commandment to restore and to build Jerusalem to the Anointed One, the prince, shall be seven weeks, and sixty-two weeks: it shall be built again, with street and moat, even in troubled times [this could be the times of struggles with the Samaritans or later with the Roman occupation, or both]. After the sixty-two weeks the Anointed One shall be cut off, and shall have nothing: and the people of the prince [prince of this world; namely, the Emperor] who shall come and shall destroy the city and the sanctuary [occurs in 70 AD]; and the end of it shall be with a flood, and even to the end shall be war; desolations are determined. He shall make a firm covenant with many for one week: and in the midst of the week he shall cause the sacrifice and the offering to cease [70 AD]; and on the wing of abominations shall come one who makes desolate; and even to the full end, and that determined, shall wrath be poured out on the desolate.

Clearly, the Messiah of Daniel is killed and the prince of this world takes control again for a time, making much spiritual desolation.

There remains much controversy over this "Pierced Messiah" passage. Hebrew is comprised primarily of consonants; vowels must be supplied by the reader. The appropriate vowels depend on the context. Thus the text may be translated as "and the Prince of the Congregation, the Branch of David, will kill him" or, alternately, as "and they killed the Prince of the Congregation, the Branch of David." Because of the second reading, the text was dubbed the "Pierced Messiah." Arguments continue, and the scrolls are complicated and use terms that are difficult to attach to specific people and events. In fact, their terms may be metaphors for many people and many events that occur in the ongoing battle between the forces of good and those of evil.

Some scholars reject the Prince of the Congregation being killed, because of other triumphant passages in the scrolls in which the Prince of the Congregation is victorious over his enemies and since the passage begins with Isaiah, a reference to Isaiah 11:1-12:

> There shall come forth a shoot from the stump of Jesse, and a branch shall grow out of his roots. And the Spirit of the Lord shall rest upon him, the spirit of wisdom and understanding, the spirit of counsel and might, the spirit of knowledge and the fear of the Lord. And his delight shall be in the fear of the Lord.
>
> He shall not judge by what his eyes see, or decide by what his ears hear; but with righteousness he shall judge the poor, and decide with equity for the meek of the earth; and he shall smite the earth with the rod of his mouth, and with the breath of his lips he shall slay the wicked. Righteousness shall be the girdle of his waist, and faithfulness the girdle of his loins. The wolf shall dwell with the lamb, and the leopard shall lie down with the kid, and the calf and the lion and the fatling together, and a little child shall lead them. The cow and the bear shall feed; their young shall lie down together; and the lion shall eat straw like the ox. The sucking child shall play over the hole of the asp, and the weaned child shall put his hand on the adder's den. They shall not hurt or destroy in all my holy mountain; for the earth shall be full of the knowledge of the Lord as the waters cover the sea. In that day the root of Jesse shall stand as an ensign to the peoples; him shall the nations seek, and his

dwellings shall be glorious. In that day the Lord will extend his hand yet a second time to recover the remnant which is left of his people, from Assyria, from Egypt, from Pathros, from Ethiopia, from Elam, from Shinar, from Hamath, and from the coastlands of the sea. He will raise an ensign for the nations, and will assemble the outcasts of Israel, and gather the dispersed of Judah from the four corners of the earth.

If this Messiah is so triumphant in the Isaiah passage to which the War Scroll refers, why then is the translation to be "they killed the Prince," rather than the "Prince killed"?

Two other challenging yet intriguing figures that appear prominently in the Dead Sea Scrolls are the "Teacher of Righteousness" and his archenemy "The Wicked Priest." The scrolls tell of the Wicked Priest attacking and killing the Teacher of Righteousness on the Day of Atonement. Scholars working on the Scrolls have assigned the role of the Teacher of Righteousness to many historical figures, most notably: Onais III; Mattathias; Zadok; Menahem; John the Baptist; and even Jesus' brother, James the Just. The Christian authorities have a problem with associating this figure with Jesus, because the Teacher of Righteousness was not divine but human, a very rare and wonderful human, but human. Was Jesus human in every respect prior to his full union with the Father (which may have occurred when commending his spirit into God's hands as he died on the cross)? If so, then Jesus, too, could be considered as one of the candidates in the search for who was the Teacher of Righteousness spoken of in the Scrolls. Of course, these two figures could be metaphors of the struggle within each soul, in which one's egocentric self assaults one's right-seeking self in a battle for dominance over consciousness and free will.

A Broader View

Of the many connections between the Essenes and early Christians, the timing of the Last Supper has to be one of the most fascinating. Biblical scholars have noticed an apparent conflict between the Gospel of Matthew and that of John's concerning the Last Supper. Matthew depicts it as having been a Passover meal, after which Jesus was arrested in the Garden, and crucified the next day (Matt. 26:17-19). John's Gospel indicates that the supper took place the day before the Passover (John 13:1 and 18:28). These two Gospel accounts are only reconciled by one amazing circumstance: the calendar used to identify this supper had to have been the Essene calendar, a solar calendar, in contrast to the lunar calendar used by the priesthood of the Temple. Using the Essene calendar, both Gospels are correct: it was a Passover meal, but it was earlier than the Temple Passover. This means that the dinner was likely held on a Thursday night, after which Jesus was arrested in the Garden, taken before a modified meeting of the Sanhedrin council, then given over to Pilate on Friday. On Friday he was crucified, died, and was buried that night. Saturday would have been the Temple Passover, and Sunday the day of Resurrection, Easter. For the two Gospel writers to matter-of-factly use the Essene solar calendar to identify the Passover rather then the Temple calendar indicates a close connection with the Essenes and their ways.

Edgar Cayce's readings of the Akashic record contain a description of the selection of young Mary as the chosen vessel for Jesus Christ. Cayce said that Mary's mother, Anna, came to the Essene Temple at Mt. Carmel. Anna explained to the Temple leaders that she had become pregnant but was still a virgin. The leaders of the Temple took Anna in, along with others they were caring for under similar circumstances. Cayce explained that the Essenes were actively attempting to prepare the way for the coming of the Messiah. They had read Genesis carefully and thereby knew that God had said Eve would conceive the redeemer of the situation that lost the Garden of Eden and direct companionship with God in the Garden. Therefore, the Essenes were looking for a female of such a spiritual consciousness and vibration that she could conceive, gestate, and birth the promised redeemer.

When Anna gave birth to a female, some of the leadership became skeptical, expecting a male child. Others countered that perhaps the vessel of the Messiah also had to be born immaculately by the Spirit of God. Therefore, Anna was considered to have been the chosen mother of the mother of the Messiah. The child, Mary, was therefore included in the training and testing of all the young girls being prepared to be the mother of the Messiah. Cayce explained that the people at the Mt. Carmel Temple were attempting to "consecrate their lives, their bodies, for a service; for a channel through which activities might be had for the perfecting, as it were, of the material channel through which such an expression of the Creative Forces might come into the earth." (Cayce, 649-2)

Mary grew in wisdom and grace. There came a day when the children were climbing the Temple steps to the altar for prayer and the burning of the incense. As they mounted the steps all the maidens were bathed in unusually bright morning sunlight; which made a beautiful sight and clothed all in purple and gold. On this day it was Mary's turn to lead the twelve chosen maidens. As Mary reached the top step, there was thunder and lightning, and the angel Gabriel appeared. The angel then led the way, taking Mary by the hand and leading her and the others to the altar. In this manner, Cayce says, the leaders of the Temple knew that Mary was the chosen maiden, and they began to prepare her for the blessed event. (Cayce, 5749-8)

Despite the uncertainty about some of the stories and names in their scrolls, the Essenes must be considered as a fertile community from which the early Christian movement began.

Another group that should be considered, though quite different than the Essenes in many ways, would be the Gnostics.

GNOSTICS

Since the discovery of the Gnostic scrolls and gospels in Nag Hammadi, Egypt, much has been made of the role of the Gnostics in the growth of spiritual understanding. Therefore, let's take a closer look at some of the key teachings in Gnosticism.

Gnosis means "knowledge" and *gnostikos* means "good at knowing"; therefore, Gnostics were "people who knew." In Gnosticism, salvation came by *knowing* the truth, and this truth would illuminate any who perceived it.

The origins of Gnosticism are difficult to pinpoint. Some believe that it began with Hermes and the "Trismegistic" literature of ancient Egypt, which reflects many Gnostic principles and stories. Others believe that it began with a blending of Persian and Babylonian religious thought, when the Persian ruler Cyrus entered Babylon in 539 BC. Many ancient tablets have been found to support this hypothesis. Still others point to the Greek aspects of Gnosticism and consider that it began with Alexander the Great and his general, Ptolemy. Others say that Gnosticism is a mystical outgrowth of Judaism, because many of the tablets unearthed in Assyria and Babylonia use terms and names of unmistakable Semitic sounds and words. Since there were many cultured Jewish colonies in the Euphrates valley (Babylon), this early origin is an understandable choice.

There is good evidence to support each of these hypotheses, so perhaps Gnosticism's roots lead back into all of these ancient cultures and locations. Whatever its origin, we know that it existed late into the fifth century

AD, and that, for some uncertain reason, all Gnostics completely adopted Christianity when it came along. This was not a localized phenomenon but spread throughout all Gnostic communities, from Spain to Persia, from Greece to Egypt. One reason ancient Gnosticism was inclined to adopt Christian thought was the fundamental belief in a savior. From very ancient times, Gnostics held that the "Good God" was going to send a powerful savior, a *Soter*, who would bring order out of chaos and open the way to salvation. Jewish messianic beliefs fit well with Gnostic views. However, several sects of the Gnostics could not accept Jehovah as an equivalent to their Good God. The Messiah prophecy they readily accepted as true, but the fierce and revengeful Jehovah was not the Lord that most Gnostics embraced.

Amazingly, and for reasons not clear from the extant literature, Gnostics accepted unequivocally that Jesus of Nazareth was indeed the long-awaited Messiah, Savior, Soter. They adopted and practiced Christian sacraments, including baptism, confirmation, communion, and a uniquely Gnostic sacrament called *Nymphon*, literally meaning "bride chamber," which was a ceremony whereby they wedded their souls to their angels, or the spiritual portion of themselves that remained in Heaven – basing this on Jesus' parable about the bridegroom (Matt. 25:1-13). So enthusiastic were the Gnostics about Christianity that they actually flooded the then world with esoteric Christian literature, including apocryphal Gospels, Acts, and Apocalypses. For the first few hundred years of Christianity, there was more Gnostic Christian literature than traditional Roman-Byzantine Christian literature. Paradoxically, the Christian Church today considers all Gnostic teachings to be non-Christian. This appears to have been the result of a desire by many Christian leaders to break completely from the past, pre-Christ period of spirituality and God-seeking and begin cleanly with the accepted Old and New Testaments. A part of this was a complete break with Judaism and Jews, even though the Christian first-fathers and the Christ himself were mostly pure Jewish, raised and trained in Judaism. One of the problems with the pre-Christ groups was their "contamination" by including many ancient human concepts and practices, some going back to the Egyptians, who the new leaders of Christianity considered to be little more than barbaric pagans.

Because of the multiplicity, complexity, and divergence of Gnostic thought, it is impractical to detail all of its teachings. It would also be a confusing collection of terms, names, and tales. The following is a summary of the most widely held and the most classical Gnostic concepts and stories.

Fundamentally, Gnosticism believes that matter, or physicality, is a deterioration of Spirit, and the whole of the universe a deprivation of the Divine Ideal. The ultimate end of all being is to overcome the grossness of matter and the physical world and return to the Mother-Father Spirit. Such a victory over matter and a return to the Creator will be inaugurated and facilitated by the appearance of the God-sent Savior. Gnostics believed that physical existence is essentially evil, resulting from a flaw or sin, and that it is the duty of every soul to overcome this material influence, escape it, and return to the Spirit-Parent.

According to Gnosticism, there was first the "Depth," which may be compared to the infinite unseen universe. Then there was the "Fullness of Being" (*bythos pleroma*), which is comparable to nonphysical components of the Cosmos, such as the *thought* of light, stars, galaxies, planets, moons, and so on – not the physical form of these, but their essence, their spirit, the thought of them. Amid these was "Non-Being God" (*ouk on theos*), an unindividualized consciousness that held it all together. This could be compared to Cayce's Universal

Consciousness. Then there was the Creator, who is called First Father (*propator*). Initial consciousness sprang from First Father's depths. First Father conceived the central Monad (*monas*), an indivisible oneness that pervades all life, seen and unseen. This Monad is comparable to the Logos, the Word – as the disciple John wrote: "In the beginning was the Word, and the Word was with God, and the Word was God. All things were made through this One." (John 1:1-3) There is a First Source (*proarche*), which may be compared to Cayce's First Cause. There is also "Unknown God" (*hagnostos theos*), sometimes called Unknown Father, and at other times, the Good God. Humankind (*anthropos*) came out of the indivisible oneness of the Monad.

From Good God (Unknown Father) emanates a number of pure spirit forces. They are called by different names, depending upon which group is teaching (some examples of these names are aions, syzygies, sonships, light-kings, and so on). For our purposes here, we'll refer to them as "Light Emanations." Even though there are many different names for them, the concept of *emanation* is common to all Gnostic sects. The number of Light Emanations varies widely, some numbering them in the thirties. Light Emanation is similar to the Egyptian concept of the one god RA (pronounced *ray*), emanating rays of light that have specific functions throughout the creation. One major Gnostic group teaches that the Light Emanations came in pairs: first, Depth and Silence, which produced Mind and Truth; these then produced Reason and Consciousness, and ultimately Man and Condition (or Circumstance).

The Light Emanations are not physical. They are purely ideals, hypostatic thought-forms of the supersensible dimensions. Together with the source from which they emanate, they form what is called "the Fullness of Being."

The story goes that the transition from nonmaterial life to material, physical life was the result of a flaw, or a passion, or even a sin in one of these Light Emanations. Of course, the Light Emanation most likely to have such a flaw was the pair Man and Condition. Many Gnostic groups teach that the flaw was indeed in the last Light Emanation. Some groups have a story akin to the Lucifer legend, in which the most beautiful Light among the emanations fell from grace, just as Lucifer, the most beautiful angel in heaven, fell from grace.

The ultimate end of all Gnosis (knowledge) is *mentanoia*, which means something like "making amends" to undo the flaw that led to material existence and returns one to the Fullness of Being.

There are many different Gnostic stories about the cosmology and creation process. Some of the richest are developed around the tales of Sophia (sometimes called *Achamoth*). She is the Light Emanation of Wisdom, specifically the "Wisdom from above" (*he ano Sophia*). But she is also a female spirit (*he kato Sophia*). In her ideal essence she is the "Lightsome Mother" (*he Meter he Photeine*). In her lower state she is the "Lustful One" (*he Prouneikos*), a once virginal goddess who fell from her original purity. A Gnostic magical chant used to protect one from corrupt emanations reveals the dual aspect of Sophia, calling upon her higher nature while subduing her lower nature: "I am a vessel more precious than the female who made you, if your mother ignores the source from whence she is. I know myself, and I know from whence I am and invoke the incorruptible Sophia, who is the Father, the Mother of your mother, who has neither father nor husband. A man-woman, born from a woman, has made you, not knowing her Mother, but thinking herself alone. But I invoke her Mother."

Sophia is the primal feminine principle in the universe and is the counterpart to the Unknown Father, who is the primal masculine principle in the universe.

One story tells how her great love for the Unknown Father drove her to seek to know him and to comprehend his greatness. However, such a realization would have ultimately meant the dissolution of her being into the immensity of his infinite nature. Fortunately, she was saved from falling into the abyss of infinity by a "Boundary Spirit." These spirits are stationed throughout the cosmos to guide, guard, and help.

After the creation began, Sophia perceived the inevitable chaos that would result as multiplicity overwhelmed oneness and endless layers of subsequent creations spun on and out from the original. To bring order to the chaos, she created the material universe and, specifically, our Solar System (*Hebdomad*), which is known as "the Seven Heavens." Therefore, she is "the mother of the seven heavens." Keep in mind that she is not physical, and the seven heavens are not in matter yet but only in spirit.

It is said that her concern over the chaos of multiplicity caused her to hurry back into the depths of the Unknown Father (but not losing herself in his immensity), and the union with him produced an offspring (while maintaining her virginal goddess condition, of course). This story has similarities to that of the Egyptian goddess Isis, who sought to conceive a messiah for Earth, also without conjugal intercourse. However, unlike Isis, who produced the messiah godling, Horus, Sophia projected a "formless substance," which some believe may have been ether, the fifth element – not one of the four physical elements: earth, water, fire, and air. As you may know, Cayce's readings correlate ether with the Akashic Records, which are on "the skein of time and space." In this way Sophia may be considered the creator of the essence that would ultimately result in the material universe and matter, including time and space.

In a story found in the *Pistis Sophia* (Chapter xxix), Sophia originally dwelt in the highest heaven (the thirteenth), but she was seduced by a demon who used a ray of light, which she mistook as an emanation from the First Father. She pursued this light. It led into Chaos below the twelve Lights (or heavens), where she was captured and imprisoned by the dark powers. This is similar to the Mayan tale of how the Lords of the Underworld tricked the Gods of Light, capturing and imprisoning them in the underworld and keeping them distracted with games and challenges which they rarely won.

After Sophia has fallen from the highest heaven and become captive in matter, the Unknown Father, the Good God, emanates two new Lights, Christ and the Holy Spirit! Christ and the Holy Spirit take hold of Sophia's "formless substance" and give it essence and form, whereupon Sophia tries to rise again to the Father, but in vain. To help her, the Unknown Father emanates the Savior, who must come down into the realms of matter and unite himself with the man Jesus, the son of Mary. Man is seen as a compound of body, soul, and spirit. His salvation consists in the return of his spirit (*pneuma*) to the Fullness of Being. However, if he is only a psychicist, not a full Gnostic, his soul (*psyche*) returns only to his Mother, not to the fullness found in the combination of the Mother and the Unknown Father.

The Savior's light illuminates predisposed souls moving down the stream of time and space, igniting the truth that lies dormant within the inner recesses of their being. The Gnostic Savior is not a man, but a Light that entered a man, Jesus, and manifested through him for all to see. The Gnostic Savior is the Holy Spirit that was in Jesus, rather than the man Jesus, a distinction that Cayce also makes: "Jesus is the man; Christ is the spirit."

The Good God is seen as the opposite of the World-Creator, or the Lord of this World who captures and imprisons souls. The Good God revealed himself to Jesus; to know Jesus and his gnosis (knowledge) is to become entirely free of the yoke of the World-Creator.

Gnostic salvation is not just an individual redemption of each soul but a cosmic process through which each soul must learn the whole truth. The process is quite structured and is associated with the planets in this Solar System – as the Cayce readings also indicate.

Sophia is the mother of the seven heavens and wisdom; therefore, when a soul finishes its journey through the seven heavens, the implication is that it has achieved sufficient gnosis to redeem itself from the captivating power of form over essence. The seven heavens, as given to us by the Gnostic writer Origen (*Contra Celsum*, VI, xxxi), are in this order: the heavenly realm of Saturn (*Jaldabaoth*, which may be interpreted as "Child of Chaos"); Jupiter (*Jao*, which may be derived from the Gnostic magical word *iao* – more on magical words later); Mars (*Sabaoth*, which is an Old Testament title meaning "God of Hosts"); Venus (*Astrophaios*, associated with the feminine principle); Sun (*Adonaios*, meaning "Lord"); Mercury (*Ailoaios* or *Ailoein*, or in Hebrew *Elohim*, meaning "God" – which indicates how highly the mind was held in Gnosticism); Moon (*Oraios*, which may simply mean "Light").

Gnostic salvation is the return of all things to what they were before the flaw in the sphere of the Light Emanations brought matter into existence and imprisoned a part of the Divine Light in the realm of darkness. The salvation process is universal and driven by forces of destiny. No one can avoid it. They can resist it and thereby achieve a lower level of illumination or even darkness, a darkness resulting from not knowing the truth.

"Primeval Human" (*Protanthropos*) occupies a prominent place in several Gnostic systems. It was an emanation from one of the Light Emanations. It is the fundamental being before its differentiation into individuals. Its helpmate is "Perfect Knowledge." It is pure mind before it was darkened by contact with matter. One text explains: "There is a blessed, incorruptible, endless light in the power of the Fullness of Being that is the Father of all things, who invoked the First Human. This First Human along with his Perfect Knowledge emits "the son of Man" (*Euterantropos*). The Son of Man is the same being as First Human but after its differentiation into individuals. Following the creation of the Son of Man, everything sinks into matter, into physical form. Subsequent to the creation of the Son of Man, Adam (*Anthropos*) is created as the fourth (some say third) individualized physical prototype. This concept may be compared to Cayce's four Root Races, each being an improved physical body over the previous. The Adamic bodies are quickly multiplied as to be occupied by descending souls coming out of the Spirit realms into matter.

In *Pistis Sophia* the Light Emanation *Jeu* is called the First Human. He is the overseer of Light, messenger of the First Precept (Rule). In the Books of Jeu this "great Man" is the King of the Light-Treasure, enthroned above all things and is the goal of all souls. He is the ideal. In several systems, including the "Evangelium Mariae," *Barbelo* (sometimes *Barbeloth*, *Barthenos*, even *Parthenos*) is the Godhead in its female aspect. Barbelo has most of the functions of the highest Sophia (*he ano Sophia*, "Wisdom from above"). It is believed that in individualized, incarnate form, she was the wife of Seth, through whom the good lineage led to the eventual birth of the Savior.

Some Gnostics considered Seth to be the father of all spiritual men (*pneumatikoi*, meaning "good with spirit"),

Abel to be the father of all psychic men (psychikoi, meaning "good with soul"), and Cain the father of all carnal men (hylikoi, meaning something akin to "good with flesh").

The Gnostics practiced many of the same sacraments as later Christians:

Baptism– All Gnostic sects had the rite of baptism, daily baptism. The ceremony included a seal or sign and an utterance, sometimes a tablet with a mystic word on it. Here are two of the phrases spoken at the moment of the baptism: "In the name of the Unknown Father of all, in the Truth, the Mother of all, in him who came down on Jesus"; or "In the name that was hidden from every divinity and lordship and truth, which Jesus the Nazarene has put on in the regions of light."

Confirmation– The anointing of a candidate with odoriferous ointment or oil is the Gnostic sacrament of initiation. There is some indication that the Gnostics did not so much intend to evoke the Holy Spirit upon the candidate as to seal him or her against the attacks of the dark forces or drive them away by "the sweet odor which is above all things" (*tes uter ta hola euodias*). The chrism (christening oil or ointment) usually came from Balsam, because it was believed that it flowed from the Tree of Life, and this tree was mystically connected with the Cross. Anointing would be accompanied with these words: "The hidden mystery in which the Cross is shown to us."

Gnostics used oil sacramentally for many things, such as healing the sick and anointing the dead. It was believed that the sacred odor of the oil rendered the dead safe and invisible to evil powers during their journey to the higher heavens.

Communion– Gnostics celebrated the "breaking of the bread." The use of salt in this rite was important to them. It is believed that the disciple Peter broke the bread of the Communion and "putting salt thereon, he gave first to the mother and then to us." The bread was always signed with the Cross. Gnostics called the bread "oblation" (*prosphora*). Curiously, Gnostics often substituted water for wine. They even had a story that at a communion led by Jesus himself, he set a fire, burned incense, set out two flasks and two cups, one with wine, the other with water, and asked the disciples to change the wine into water for the baptism. This is a strange twist on Jesus' changing the water into wine at the wedding and may be due to the Gnostic's belief in the fundamental evil of flesh and blood, water being preferred, as it was a symbol of life and cleansing.

All Gnostics believed in and practiced magic. They had numerous magic spells, amulets, chants, charms, and diagrams. They believed that the seven vowels were powerful magic. Uttering them or having them written on a tablet or amulet called forth their power and protection. Each vowel represented one of the seven heavens, and the whole of them reflected the Universe. Without consonants, they represented the Ideal and Infinite not yet imprisoned and limited by matter. They also represented a musical scale, and many a Gnostic sheet of vowels was in fact a sheet of music, each vowel representing a note.

Diagrams were also magical. Circles within circles, squares, parallel lines, and so on, were considered to represent aspects of the Cosmos. These were often combined with mathematical figures and names written within them. The universe was symbolized by a triangle enclosed in a circle.

The number 3 was the key to all mysteries. The three supreme principles are these: not-created, self-created, and created. The Savior has a threefold nature, a threefold body, threefold powers, and so on. Of course, the triangle has three sides, and in the diagram of the universe it represents the triune condition within the infinite circle. In this way multiplicity has been contained in a trinity, making it easier to know and regain the lost oneness.

As we leave the Gnostics and their role in the story of Christ and Christianity, it is important to keep in mind that there were numerous Gnostic groups, each with its own variations of these concepts, stories, names, and terms. Gnostic writings were voluminous and complex, even confusing. What has been presented here is a distillation of its most relevant and helpful ideas.

A Broader View

Chapter Four
THE JOURNEY OF CHRISTIANITY

THE EMPIRE AND THE CHURCH

In the early years after Jesus Christ's ascension, the Romans did not initially distinguish between Judean Jews and Christians. Both were lumped together as troublemakers. However, Jews in the Diaspora were accepted by Rome as members of a legal religion, with formal approval to practice their faith. But in Judea, the Romans brutally crushed the Jews, including the Christian Jews, during the war of 63 AD to 70 or until Masada in 73. After this war there was no Jewish Nation, no Temple. What David had begun roughly a thousands years ago, the Romans destroyed. And the Nation of Israel would not appear again for nearly another thousand years.

Eventually, Rome began to identify Christians as a specific group, separate from Jews. Paradoxically, the Roman Empire considered Christians to be godless, because their religion did not fit into any of the politically sanctioned faiths. They also considered Christians to be part of a cult that held to some kind of cannibalism (eating the body and blood of their founder, even if only symbolically). From a Roman perspective, Christians also appeared to have a persecution complex – seeking public martyrdom with a passion – something the Romans were happy to provide. Faced with Christians offering themselves for persecution with such willingness, while seeking no accommodation for their faith from the Roman authorities, Rome established a systematic process of public Christian executions, deaths in the arena, punitive labor in the mines, confiscation of property, and banishment. For two hundred years these persecutions were a part of the Roman power machine. The psychological effect of these persecutions on the Roman public was not understood by the authorities until it was too late. But future anti-Christian powers, such as National Socialism and Communism, avoided public martyrdom, shifting instead to nighttime raids that led to imprisonment, concentration camps, and secret murders.

These early times were hard times for Christians. A fragment of an interesting letter addressed to Bishop Soter, the Bishop of Rome from 167 to 175, by Dionysius of Corinth provides us with some insights into these times. Note his comment about aiding the Christians laboring in the Roman mines: "From the beginning it has been your custom to do good to all the brethren in many ways, and to send alms to many churches in every city, refreshing the poverty of those who sent requests, or giving aid to the brethren in the mines by the alms which you have had the habit of giving from old, Romans keeping up the traditional custom of the Romans; which your blessed Bishop Soter has not only preserved, but has even increased, by providing the abundance which he has sent to the saints, and by further consoling with blessed words with brethren who came to him, as a loving father his children. Today, therefore, we have kept the holy Lord's day, on which we have read your letter, which we shall always have to read and be admonished, even as the former letter which was written to us by the ministry of Clement." (Eusebius, *Historical Ecclesiastica*, IV, xxiv.)

But a miracle was about to happen, a miracle that would significantly improve the lives of Christians. And, as with so much of the work of the Holy Spirit, this miracle would be done to a nonbeliever, but a very, very important nonbeliever. In 306, Flavius Valerius Aurelius Constantinus, better known as Constantine, became emperor of the Roman Empire. He made his headquarters in the great and ancient city of Byzantium, whose name he changed to Constantinople. This Eastern city is located on the Bosphorus Strait, which separates Europe from Asia. It is modern-day Istanbul.

When Maxentius, the son of a former Roman Emperor, brought armies from Rome against Constantine to challenge his rule over the entire Empire, both the Eastern and Western territories, Constantine had a dream the night before the battle. In this dream he was directed to put the sign of the Christ on his soldiers' shields if he wanted to be victorious. He did so, and on October 28, 312, he defeated Maxentius' armies at the Battle of the Milvian Bridge. This story was first told by the live-in tutor of Constantine's son; who would have had a unique position by which to hear the dream and the activities firsthand. Twenty-five years later, a more elaborate form of this story was developed and written in *Life of Constantine* by Eusebius.

Constantine then publicly claimed that his victory was due to the power of the God of the Christians. He became a Christian and supported the faith from that day on. There are those who believe that his conversion was motivated more by political necessities than religious feelings, but the historical evidence does not support such an opinion. Constantine became a Christian because of his personal experience with the God of the Christians. He did not know much about the faith, possibly never fully understood it, but he had experienced its power and threw the full weight of his imperial power behind Christianity.

An alliance between the Eastern and Western Roman Empire was formed between Constantine and Maxentius' successor, Licinius, in Milan, Italy. At this time (313) they also signed the Edict of Milan, which gave all Christians the legal right to practice their religion. But Licinius never became a Christian and never honored the Edict. In 320 he began to persecute Christians and Christian sympathizers. In 324 Licinius moved against Constantine in an effort to take control of both the Eastern and Western Roman Empire, but Constantine defeated him. Nevertheless, in Rome and the Western Empire, Christians were not as protected and free as they were in the Eastern Empire. While the Edict of Milan also protected Jews and is also known as the "Edict of Toleration," Judaism was seen as a rival to Christianity, and among other measures, Constantine forbade the conversion of pagans to Judaism.

Constantine not only granted the Christian Church freedom to practice their faith, he united the Church with the Empire. The Church became a partner with the new *Christian* Empire. This partnership began in the Byzantine Empire (fourth-fifth centuries), continued in the Carolingian Empire of the Franks (eighth-ninth centuries), and culminated in the medieval Holy Roman Empire of the German nation, which lasted until Napoleon dissolved the imperial unity in 1806.

Byzantium (later Constantinople; today, Istanbul) was the capital of the Eastern Roman Empire. Its location in Asia Minor (modern Turkey) was ideal for the young Christian Church, whose seven major churches were located in Asia Minor, as listed in the Revelation: Ephesus, Smyrna, Pergamum, Thyatira, Sardis, Philadelphia, and Laodicea. From Byzantium, now Constantinople, the movement found its way into the Western Roman Empire, and eventually to Rome itself. However, the Byzantine, or Eastern Orthodox, Church never accepted or submitted to the Roman Papacy. It took a different course than the Roman Christian Church, Catholicism, retaining many of the features, liturgy, and tenets of the early church.

In AD 325 Constantine assembled 318 bishops, each elected by his community, at Nicaea, in Bithynia, to debate and affirm some principles of their faith. The result, known as the Nicene Creed, is now part of the Roman Catholic Mass and the Anglican churches' service of Communion. It is as follows:

The Nicene Creed

We believe in one God the Father, the Almighty, maker of heaven and earth, of all that is, seen and unseen. We believe in one Lord, Jesus Christ, the only Son of God, eternally begotten of the Father, God from God, Light from Light, true God from true God, begotten, not made, of one Being with the Father; through him all things were made. For us and for our salvation he came down from heaven, was incarnate of the Holy Spirit and the Virgin Mary and became truly human. For our sake he was crucified under Pontius Pilate; he suffered death and was buried. On the third day he rose again in accordance with the Scriptures; he ascended into heaven and is seated at the right hand of the Father. He will come again in glory to judge the living and the dead, and his kingdom will have no end. We believe in the Holy Spirit, the Lord, and the giver of life, who proceeds from the Father and the Son, who with the Father and the Son is worshiped and glorified, who has spoken through the prophets. We believe in the one holy catholic [in the sense of "universal"] and apostolic church. We acknowledge one baptism for the forgiveness of sins. We look for the resurrection of the dead, and the life of the world to come. Amen.

The Formal Service: Mass

The first indication that the new Christians had developed a formal ceremony may be found in Paul's I Corinthians 10:21, where he contrasts the "table of the Lord" (*trapeza*

Kyriou), on which the Eucharist is offered, with the "table of devils," or pagan altars. Paul's letter to the Hebrews, 13:10, refers to the Christian altar as *thysiasterion*, the word by which the Septuagint alludes to Noah's altar.

Early on, Greek was the Christian language, in the East as well as in Rome. Therefore, *Eucharistia*, was the term for the consecrated bread and wine. But it was also the word used for the whole service. Clement of Rome (who died about 101) used the verbal form, meaning "giving thanks." Justin Martyr (who died about 167) speaks of *eucharist* repeatedly. Subsequently, the word has always been used. It remains the common name for the consecrated bread and wine. Clement calls the service *Leitourgia*, with, however, a shade of different meaning: "rite" or "oblation." In the third century, Latin began to take over. While *eucharistia* remained very common, we also find *gratiarum actio, sacrificium*, generally with *divina sacrificia, novum sacrificium, sacrificia Dei*. We find also *Solemnia, Spirituale ac coeleste sacramentum, Dominicum, Officium*, even *Passio*, and other expressions that are rather descriptions than technical names. Eventually and continuing today, the bread and wine, symbolizing the body and blood of Christ, is the Eucharist, and the service is the Mass.

The Roman Catholic Church traces its origin to St. Augustine and synods of the sixth century, in which "dismissal" of the congregation after the sermon became "mass." In Latin, *Missa Catechumenorum* means the dismissal of the catechumens. For some reason, the people began to refer to the service as the "dismissal" or *missa*. However, there are other possibilities, many of which seem more likely. For example, *missa* may have originated from the Hebrew *missah*, meaning "oblation." It may have come from the Greek *myesis*, meaning "initiation." It may come from the German *Mess*, meaning "assembly."

A Broader View

In the *Daily Missal of the Mystical Body* edited by the Maryknoll Fathers, a Mass is defined as a ceremony in which a priest and an assembly of the "royal priesthood" or "holy nation" of the people "cooperate in the building of a mystical reality that embraces heaven and earth, the Incarnate Word, and all mankind, living and dead...." We, the people, as a "royal priesthood" is a concept from I Peter 2:9. The union through the Mass is expressed in Jesus' prayer at the Last Supper: "Holy Father, I pray that all may be one, even as thou, Father, in me and I in thee; that they also may be one in us." (John 17:11-12) The Mass is modeled after the Last Supper. It contains the acts of breaking bread and drinking wine together, the bread representing a mystical breaking of the Earthly body's hold on us and the drinking of wine, the offering of blood as a symbolic sacrifice of our will in deference to God's. These acts actually began with the High Priest Melchizedek, when he met Abram returning from rescuing his brother, Lot, from captivity. Melchizedek broke bread and served wine to celebrate Abram's act of concern for another, caring more about easing his brother's suffering than his own personal safety and peace (Gen. 18:14-20). Edgar Cayce identified Melchizedek as one of the incarnations of the Logos (Cayce, 262-55, 364-7). Jesus was another. Interestingly, one of Jesus' first acts on the Sunday of his resurrection was to break bread with two disciples in Emmaus, instantly revealing to them who he really was (Luke 24:30-31).

In the first century the Mass was practiced in secret. Lacking churches, the faithful met in homes or secret places, usually near tombs of martyrs, such as the Catacombs. In 107 AD, St. Ignatius of Antioch writes of a unique Mass conducted upon a consecrated altar just before his arrest and martyrdom in Rome. In 180 AD, Aberico, Bishop of Geropolis, made a voyage from Asia Minor to Rome. His diary records that along the way "everywhere were found brethren joined together" in communion meetings. In the second century St. Justin writes of secret gatherings: "whether dwelling in the city or in the country" the faithful gathered "in the same place" for Communion.

The people came to believe that when they ingested the bread and the wine, they were ingesting the mystical body and blood of Christ, the Messiah. This cleansed and strengthened them for the trials of life. As time passed, the ceremony became more elaborate, with special prayers and hymns – mostly in Latin. For example, the preparatory prayers said at the altar were these: *In nomine Patris, et Filii, et Spiritus Sancti. Amen. Introibo ad altare Dei.* "In the Father's name, and the Son's, and the Holy Spirit's. Amen. I will go in to the altar of God." *Emitte lucem tuam, et veritatem tuam; ipsa me deduxerunt, et adduxerunt in montem sanctum tuum, et in tabernacula tua.* "Send forth your light and your truth; they shall lead me on and bring me to your holy mountain, and to your dwelling place (tabernacle)."

These were followed by activities leading up to the breaking of bread and drinking of wine together. Here's a common sequence: 1. Entrance Hymn, 2. Preparatory prayer (a portion quoted above), 3. Reading from scripture, 4. Testament of faith (Nicene Creed), 5. Offering and Sharing, 6. Offertory prayer and hymn, 7. Silent or Secret Prayer, 8. Blessing or consecrating the bread and wine, 9. Communion.

A typical offertory prayer was this: *Jubilate Deo, omnis terra; servite Domino in laetitia; intrate in conspectu ejus in exsultatione, quia Dominus ipse est Deus.* "Sing joyfully to God, all the earth; serve the Lord with gladness; come before him with joyful song, for the Lord is God." A typical silent or secret prayer was this: *Ab occultis meis munda me, Domine, et ab alientis parce servo tuo.* "Cleanse me from my hidden faults, Lord, and spare your servants from those of others." The call to spare us from faults of others is an interesting approach.

As the church grew, the ceremony became structured. Bells and incense were added. Special vessels were designed. Vestments of colors were chosen to represent sacred anniversaries. White is the color for Christmas Mass, representing innocence, purity, and victory. Red symbolizes sacrifice, used during Masses for martyrs. Purple is penitence, used during Advent and Lent. Green is for hope, used at Masses following Epiphany and Pentecost. Old Rose is subdued joy, used at times during Advent and Lent. Black is for mourning, used at Masses for the dead.

The important principle is union through communion. The Christ-*mass* creates a sense of oneness among one another as we come together in love and sharing, as we break bread and drink wine in memory of the oneness of the Father and the Son. Mystically this creates the Holy Spirit within and among us, uniting us in the truth that all is one. *Deus qui inhabitare facit unanimes in domo:* "God makes man to dwell in unity in his house."

Returning now to the journey of Christianity, in the West, the Roman Christian Church began much differently than in the Near East. In the West, secret communities were formed in the heart of the Western Empire capital of Rome. The Roman Catholic Church traces its popes back to the apostle Peter through the line of the Bishops of Rome, beginning with Bishop Linus, who reigned as Bishop of Rome from about 64 AD to 76. This Linus is believed to be the one mentioned in Paul's II Timothy 4:21: "Do your best to come before winter. Eubu'lus sends greetings to you, as do Pudens and Linus and Claudia and all the brethren." AD 64 is believed to be the same year that the disciples Peter and Paul were executed in Rome. Paul was in prison for two years awaiting his execution. During this time we know that he met and taught many, presumably

Linus would have been among them. Therefore, the Roman Church claims that it was founded by Peter and Paul.

The disciples of Jesus Christ spread out in many different directions, some by force of captivity, Peter for example, others by choice. The disciple John was with the church community in Ephesus, along with Jesus' mother and some of the other Holy Women (Mary Magdalene, Elois, and others). Andrew journeyed farther north, into Byzantium. The disciple and gospel writer Mark journeyed south, into Egypt, and founded the Coptic Christian Church. The Coptic Church retains many of the same early characteristics as the Eastern Orthodox Church. The Greek and Russian Orthodox Churches also retain the Eastern ways. It is believed that Thomas, known for his discussion with Jesus at the Last Supper (John 14:5) and his doubting of Jesus' resurrection (John 20:27), journeyed Eastward into Persia and India.

When Rome was conquered by the Franks (Germanic peoples) at the end of the fifth century, the Western Emperor's capital was no longer Rome. Constantinople was considered to be the new Rome. During this time of confusion in Italy, the Bishops of Rome enhanced their power and stature. In one seemingly scandalous event, the Bishop of Rome conferred the title of Emperor upon the Frankish prince! An action that the Church, centered in Constantinople, supposedly the center of the Empire and Christianity, considered to be illegal and rebellious. As the Rome-centered Western Church grew in influence, the Byzantine and Roman Churches held relatively equal positions in Christendom. Throughout this period the Byzantine wing of the Christian Church struggled to hold on to its premier position as the first Christian center and claimed that it had been founded by the "first disciple," Andrew. It was Andrew who first saw Jesus after his baptism in the Jordan River, and it was Andrew who learned from John the Baptist that Jesus was indeed the prophesied Messiah. Andrew later told his brother Peter and led him to Jesus. In the ninth century, the Byzantine patriarch Photius (858-886) began to distance his congregation from the Roman-led communities, arguing that the bishops of Rome had fallen away from the faith. These two major arms of Christianity separated into distinctly different organizations. The Bishops of Rome became the Popes and began to build the Roman Catholic Church, with its center in Rome. The Eastern Orthodox Christian Church maintained its center in Constantinople.

But a new threat rose in the East, one that would stop the expansion and reduce the influence of Christianity, both Roman Catholic and Eastern Orthodox, until the 1700s. In 630 AD, Muhammad, or Mohammed, the rasul, or "messenger," prophet of Islam, and his army conquered Mecca. He united the tribes of Arabia into a vast army to conquer the world for Allah. His death in 632 did not lessen the fervor of his followers. The first *caliph*, meaning "deputy of the prophet," Abu Bakr, ambitiously undertook a series of military conquests to spread the new faith across the world. Although he died two years later, his nephew, Umar, continued the ambitious program. In 636, the Muslims conquered and occupied Jerusalem, Damascus, and Antioch. In 646, the Muslims conquered Egypt, which ended the growth of Coptic Christianity. The Muslims quickly spread across northern Africa, and from Morocco, they invaded Christian Spain in 711.

In 1453 Muslim Turks conquered Constantinople and all of Asia Minor. The spiritual center of Christianity for the past eleven hundred years, Constantinople, became Islamic. It's Imperial Christian Church became a mosque, and the city's name was changed to Istanbul. However, Eastern Orthodox Christianity did not completely disappear. The Greeks were able to maintain their orthodox form of Christianity, though they lost all their holdings in Asia Minor. The main body of the Eastern

Orthodox Church was adopted by the Russian princes of Moscow. Moscow became the new Rome of the Eastern Empire, and their leaders took the title of *Tzar*, meaning "Caesar." Moscow became the new center of Orthodox Christianity for the next five hundred years, until the Bolshevik revolution of October 1917, "Red October" as it is known. Amazingly, the loss of the Russian Christian Church was prophesied by Mary, the mother of Jesus, during an apparition weeks earlier on October 13, 1917, in Fatima, Portugal. The Bolshevik atheistic communists crushed the Christian movement in Russia and Eastern Europe until, synchronistically, Christmas Day 1991, when the Union of Soviet Socialist Republics (U.S.S.R.) collapsed and the Eastern Orthodox Church was free again.

The invasions and threats from the armies of Islam naturally created anti-Islamic feelings, but surprisingly, they also generated anti-Semitism for all Semites, Arabs, of course, but also Jews! Christians lumped the Jews in with the Muslim Semites.

THE CHRISTIAN INQUISITION

The threat of Islam was a challenge to Christianity from the East. An even greater challenge came from within the faith itself. Today, it is not the threat it was, but at the time, it became a fever that very nearly killed the religion and left a terrible mark. The Inquisition was a formal movement charged with finding and eradicating heresies. We think of it as a middle-ages event, but this can be traced all the way back to the early Synods in Constantinople. Later, it became an institution in the hierarchical and centralized bureaucracy of the Roman Catholic Church. But it appeared very early in the journey of Christianity.

As the early Church increased its centralization and control, doctrinal arguments were settled by Church Councils, beginning with the Council of Nicea in 325, which formulated the Nicene Creed. Some necessary and good work came out of these formal gatherings, but they also produced some deadly results. When beliefs or practices deviated sufficiently from the orthodoxy of the councils, they became the object of investigation and persecution. Heresies (from Latin *haeresis*, meaning "sects" or "schools of belief") were a problem for the Church from the beginning. In the early centuries there were the Arians and Manicheans; in the Middle Ages there were the Cathari and Waldenses; and in the Renaissance there were the Hussites, Lutherans, Calvinists, and Rosicrucians. All were movements that the central Church saw as threats to the pure truth as they saw it. And since the Councils were the keepers of the true faith, other ideas and teachers needed to be extinguished.

This type of central authority and intolerance for any deviations from the accepted view caused the death of many Christians. More Christians have been killed by Christians than all those killed by Rome in the years of persecution. For example, Edward Gibbon, in *The History of the Decline and Fall of the Roman Empire*, concludes that about 2,000 Christians were martyred by Rome, whereas 3,150 Christians were killed in a single-day sectarian argument between the followers of Arius and Athanasius, over whether Christ was part of the Trinity of the Godhead or created by Father-God. Arius, a priest from Alexandria, Egypt, who took the position that the Father created the Son, the Christ, was condemned as a heretic at the Council of Nicaea in 325, before "the most pious emperor Constantine." *Anathema* became the formal word of condemnation for any teaching or thought that was heretical to Church doctrine.

There is evidence that the journeys of young Jesus to the Eastern World was removed during one or more of these Synods, because it tainted the new faith with doctrines that were considered pagan. It is highly unlikely that the writers of the Gospels did not know anything about Jesus' early years, prior to his ministry. There had to have been journals with this part of the story of Jesus.

There is also evidence that the concept of reincarnation, or a form of it, may have been an accepted teaching of Christianity for about five hundred years. At the Synod of 543, the Emperor Justinian presented a paper against the writings of Origen (185-254 AD), whose work contained many insights into the idea of preexistence of the soul, prior incarnation of the soul, and karma. Origen wrote in his *De Principiis*: "Every soul...comes into this world strengthened by the victories or weakened by the defeats of its previous life. Its place in this world as a vessel appointed to honor or dishonor, is determined by its previous merits or demerits. Its work in this world determines its place in the world which is to follow this."

Now Origen was among the early Christian teachers and authors. He had been dead since 254, but his writings were still widely read, enough to make him a target of the Emperor. At the Synod of 553 in Constantinople, Origen's works were found "anathema" and expunged from church doctrine.

The Eastern Church, with its Greek background, had a deep understanding of these metaphysical philosophies. Here's a well-known example from Plato: "Know that if you become worse you will go to the worse souls, and if better, to the better souls; and in every succession of life and death you will do and suffer what like must fitly suffer at the hands of like." –Plato (582-507 BC), *The Republic*

Clement of Alexandria (150-220 AD) was a highly regarded early Christian, later becoming a saint. He wrote: "We were in being long before the foundation of the world; we existed in the eye of God, for it is our destiny to live in Him. We are reasonable creatures of the Divine Word; therefore we have existed from the beginning, for in the beginning was the Word."

St. Gregory (257-332 AD) wrote: "It is absolutely necessary that the soul should be healed and purified, and if this does not take place during its life on earth, it must be accomplished in future lives."

St. Augustine (354-430 AD) wrote: "The message of Plato, the purest and the most luminous of all philosophy, has at last scattered the darkness of error, and now shines forth mainly in Plotinus, a Platonist so like his master that one would think they lived together, or rather – since so long a period of time separates them – that Plato was born again in Plotinus."

Beyond the teachings and ideas of these early church fathers, we actually find passages in the Bible which may indicate a knowledge and acceptance of reincarnation. Here are a few examples.

In Proverbs 8:22-30 we find this passage: "The Lord possessed me in the beginning of his way, before his works of old. I was set up from everlasting, from the beginning, or ever the earth was. When there were no depths, I was brought forth; when there were no fountains abounding with water. Before the mountains were settled, before the hills was I brought forth: While as yet he had not made the earth, nor the fields, nor the highest part of the dust of the world. When he prepared the heavens, I was there: when he set a compass upon the face of the depth: When he established the clouds above: when he strengthened the fountains of the deep: When he gave to the sea his decree, that the waters should not pass his commandment: when he appointed the fountains of the earth: Then I was by him, as one brought up with him."

We've already seen the passages referring to John the Baptist as the reincarnation of Elijah. Here they are again for review: "Behold, I will send you Elijah the prophet, before the day when the Lord comes." –Malachi 4:5

"An angel of the Lord appeared to him, standing on the right side of the altar of incense. Zacharias was troubled when he saw him, and fear fell upon him. But the angel said to him, 'Don't be afraid, Zacharias, because your request has been heard, and your wife, Elizabeth, will bear you a son, and you shall call his name John. You will have joy and gladness; and many will rejoice at his birth. For he will be great in the sight of the Lord, and he will drink no wine nor strong drink. He will be filled with the Holy Spirit, even from his mother's womb. He will turn many of the children of Israel to the Lord, their God. He will go before him *in the spirit and power of Elijah*, "to turn the hearts of the fathers to the children," and the disobedient to the wisdom of the just; to make ready a people prepared for the Lord.'" –Luke 1:13-17 (My italics, and the quote that follows the italics is from Malachi 4:5-6: "Behold, I will send you Elijah the prophet before the great and terrible day when Lord comes. He will *turn the hearts of the fathers to the children*, and the hearts of the children to their fathers, lest I come and strike the earth with a curse." Zacharias, a priest, would have definitely known this passage and its implications about his coming son.)

"His disciples asked him, saying, 'Then why do the scribes say that Elijah must come first?' Jesus answered them, 'Elijah indeed comes first, and will restore all things, but I tell you that Elijah has come already, and they didn't recognize him, but did to him whatever they wanted to. Even so the Son of Man will also suffer by them.' Then the disciples understood that he spoke to them of John the Baptizer." –Matthew 17:9-13

"For all the prophets and the law prophesied until John. If you are willing to receive it, this is Elijah, who is to come. He who has ears to hear, let him hear." –Matthew 11:13-14

Here's a passage that clearly indicates that the disciples understood that conditions in this life may have come from prior activity: "As Jesus passed by, he saw a man which was blind from his birth. And His disciples asked Him, saying, "Master, who did sin, this man or his parents; that he was *born blind*?" –John 9:1-2 (my italics)

"Him that overcometh will I make a pillar in the temple of the Lord, *and he shall go no more out.*" – Revelation 3:12 (my italics)

But Justinian and others considered these ideas to be a distraction to the main mission and message of Christianity and an unacceptable tie to old pagan faiths that needed to be completely expunged from this new faith.

Beginning in the 12th century, Church Councils required secular rulers to prosecute heretics. In 1231, Pope Gregory IX published a decree which called for life imprisonment with beneficial penance for the heretic who had confessed and repented but capital punishment for those who persisted. The secular authorities were to carry out the execution. Pope Gregory relieved the bishops and archbishops of this obligation and made it the duty of the Dominican Order. By the end of the decade, the Inquisition had become a general institution in all lands under the purview of the Pope. By the end of the 13th centuries, the Inquisition in each region had a bureaucracy of its own. The inquisitor could bring charges against anyone. The accused had to testify against him- or herself (many more women were charged than men) and had no right to question the accuser. It was acceptable to take testimony from criminals, persons of bad reputation, excommunicated people, and heretics. The accused did not have any right to counsel, and blood relationship did not exempt one from the duty to testify against the accused. Sentences could not be appealed. Sometimes inquisitors interrogated entire populations in their jurisdiction. The inquisitor was required to question the accused in the presence of at least two witnesses. The accused was given a summary of the charges and had to take an oath to tell the truth. Various means were used to get the cooperation of the accused. Although there was no tradition of torture in Christian canon law, torture came into use by the middle of the 13th century. The findings of the Inquisition were read before a large audience; the penitents recanted on their knees with one hand on a Bible held by the inquisitor. Penalties ranged from visits to churches, pilgrimages, and wearing the cross of infamy, to imprisonment (usually for life, but the sentences were often commuted), and if the accused would not recant, then they were put to death by burning at the stake – carried out by the secular authorities. In some serious cases when the accused had died before proceedings could be instituted, his or her remains could be exhumed and burned. Death or life imprisonment was always accompanied by the confiscation of all the accused's property.

In the Spain of Ferdinand and Isabella, the chief threat of heresy was thought to proceed from the Jews, *conversos* (Jews converted to Christianity), and the Islamic Moors. The Spanish Inquisition's motivation was the national passion for "purity of blood." The Iberian peninsula was unique in medieval Europe in that it had a mixed population of Christians, Moslems, and Jews. For centuries the Spanish had been more tolerant of Jews than many other Christian nations. Jews entered trades and professions and mingled freely with Gentiles. The Fourth Lateran Council, called by Pope Innocent III in 1215, urged the enactment of laws against Jews. From the thirteenth century onward, such anti-Semitic legislation became common in Spain, though the Jews were powerful enough to prevent it from being rigorously enforced. In learning, the professions, government and administration, and finance, they had risen to positions of great importance. During the Christian reconquest of Spain from the Moors, they were indispensable. But racial feelings against the

Moors strangely included the Jews. In 1391 Jews were massacred throughout Spain on an unprecedented scale. In Seville alone four thousand were killed, and the total number of victims may have reached fifty thousand. Many Jews, to save their lives, became Christians. With further massacres and anti-Semitic laws, the process of conversion was hastened. The *New Christians*, another term for the conversos, escaped the limitations placed on Jews and thus were again able to rise to leading positions in both church and state. High offices came to be held by men who had Jewish blood. A large number married into the aristocracy, to the point where many, perhaps most, of the noble families of Spain had received some mixture of Jewish blood. Ferdinand himself had Jewish blood.

Because of the intense feeling of the Spanish about purity of blood, the prestige and privileges of the nobility were threatened. The Inquisition arose partly from the desire of the nobles to preserve their position by stamping out the threat of racial contamination. In 1492, after the fall of Granada, the authorities decreed that all Jews in Spain must either be baptized or leave the country. Estimates as to the numbers involved vary greatly. Anywhere from 165,000 to 400,000 may have left; perhaps 50,000 remained and became converted. Thus there were officially no Jews in Spain after 1492. The Moslems' turn came in 1525 when Charles V ordered the expulsion of all Moors from the territories of Aragon by the end of January 1526.

Mass burnings on the Iberian peninsula were known as *autos-de-fé*, "acts of faith." They were held once a month on the average, usually on a Sunday or holiday so all could attend; to stay away was thought suspicious. Sometimes the spectators were invited to participate in the diversion known as "shaving the new Christians." This meant setting fire to the hair or beards of those waiting their turn at the stake.

Pope Paul III established, in 1542, a permanent congregation staffed with cardinals and other officials, whose task it was to maintain and defend the integrity of the faith and to examine and proscribe errors and false doctrines. This body, the Congregation of the Holy Office, now called the Congregation for the Doctrine of the Faith, part of the Roman Curia, became the supervisory body of local Inquisitions. The Pope himself holds the title of prefect but never exercises this office. Instead, he appoints one of the cardinals to preside over the meetings. There are usually ten other cardinals on the Congregation as well as a prelate and two assistants all chosen from the Dominican Order. The Holy Office also has an international group of consultants, experienced scholars of theology and canon law, who advise it on specific questions. In 1616 these consultants gave their assessment of the new scientific propositions that the Earth moves around Sun, judging such to be "foolish and absurd in philosophy," and to be "at least erroneous in faith" in theology. This assessment led to Copernicus' *De Revolutionibus Orbium Coelestium* being placed on the Index of Forbidden Books, until revised, and Galileo to be admonished about his Copernicanism. It was this same body in 1633 that tried Galileo.

Single women were particularly vulnerable to the inquisitor's hunt for evil and heresy. In Christianity, the Garden of Eden story created a suspicion of women as being inherently evil or at least more vulnerable to the Devil's powers, and a danger to men. Jews, who first wrote and retained this story for centuries, never took this view of the story. In point of fact, in Genesis, the Lord actually speaks directly to Eve, saying that out of her will come the redeemer of this fall from Grace. But for some reason, Christian men could not get it out of their minds that Eve brought Adam into her sin with the Devil. This deep, often subliminal, belief colored the all-male inquisitors' judgment for centuries. In many ways, it continues today. But during the Inquisition, this belief caused countless women to be accused unfairly and suffer cruel brutality. The chronicler of Trèves reported that in the year 1586, except for two women, the entire female population of two villages was wiped out by the inquisitors. In 1589, 133 people, mostly women, were burned in a single day at Quedlinburg, Germany. Henri Boguet, inquisitorial judge and author of *Discours des sorciers*, a guide to catching sorceresses, reported that in 1590 Germany was "almost entirely occupied with building fires (for witches); and Switzerland has been compelled to wipeout many of her villages on their (witches') account. Travelers in Lorraine may see thousands and thousands of the stakes to which witches are bound."

In 1524, it is estimated that one thousand women accused of being witches died at Como, Italy. In Strasbourg, France, over a period of twenty years, approximately five thousand women were burned at the stake. The Senate of Savoy, a duchy lying between Italy and France, condemned 800 women at one time. Nicholas Remy (1530-1612) wrote that he personally sentenced 900 women in 15 years and in one year alone forced sixteen women to suicide. A Bishop of Nancy, France, claimed to have burned over 800 women in 16 years. One of the bishops of Würzburg, Germany, claimed over 1,900 in 5 years. Five hundred were burned alive in a three-month period in Geneva, Switzerland. Four hundred were executed in a single day in Toulouse, France. The city of Trèves is said to have burned at least 7,000 women as witches!

Wholesale burnings in Germany are suggested by the observation of a visitor to the town of Wolfenbuttel, Germany, in 1590: "There were so many stakes to burn the witches that the place of execution resembled a small forest." The executioner of Neisse in Silesia (Central Europe) invented an oven in which he roasted to death forty-two women and young girls in one year. Within nine years he had roasted over a thousand women, including children two- to four years old.

This wasn't confined to Roman Catholics; the Lutheran prelate Benedict Carpzov (1595-1666), who claimed to have read the Bible 53 times, sentenced 20,000 "devil-worshipping" women to death!

Even relatively permissive England, which never formally institutionalized the Inquisition, killed some 30,000 women as witches between 1542 and 1736.

Finally, we cannot leave the Inquisition without mentioning the assault against Christian mystics. Many Christians who sought direct contact with God and God's revelation upon them personally were seen as threats to the ordinances and authorities of the formal, centralized Church. Many of these genuine Christians were caught up in the Inquisition and executed.

This shameful slaughter and bloody mark on Christianity went on throughout Europe for nearly five hundred years! One can only imagine the karma created by such ungodly acts.

THE PROTESTANT REFORMATION

The basis of the Protestant Reformation was laid out by the German Augustinian monk Martin Luther (1483–1546), a Professor of Theology at the University of Wittenberg, Saxony. In 1517, Luther nailed to a church door in Wittenberg a manifesto listing 95 Theses against the selling of indulgences, which essentially allowed sinners to buy their way into heaven. Luther also questioned basic tenets of the Roman Catholic Church, including the clergy's exclusive right to grant salvation. He believed human salvation depended on individual faith, not on clerical mediation, and conceived of the Bible as the ultimate and sole source of Christian truth. He also advocated the abolition of monasteries and criticized the church's materialistic use of art. Luther was excommunicated in 1520 but was granted protection by the elector of Saxony, Frederick the Wise (1463–1525), and given protection in Wartburg.

Luther first despaired that humans were incurably evil by nature and could not do enough "good works" to be saved. As he studied the Epistles of Paul, he found new inspiration that led him to teach a doctrine based on three revolutionary principles: 1. By faith alone (*Sola fide*), 2. By scripture alone (*Sola scriptura*), and 3. By grace alone (*Sola gratia*).

In Romans 1:17, Luther found Paul's teaching, "The just shall live by faith," and he concluded that humans can gain salvation through faith, rather than through "good works" or the dispensations of the Church. Until the Reformation, the Church had a monopoly on God's grace, which was dispensed through the sacraments and guaranteed by the granting of indulgences. The doctrine of justification by faith alone removed the need for a priestly hierarchy to mediate between God and the individual.

When he realized that religious truth could be known through reading the Word of God as revealed in the Bible, it opened the door for God's Word to be the guiding authority, not Catholic doctrines and rituals which had uncertain Scriptural support.

In Paul's Ephesians 2:8-9, Luther found the power of Grace: "For by grace are ye saved, through faith, and that not of yourselves: it is the gift of God: Not of works, lest any man should boast." Luther came to believe that through God's mysterious grace, an elect few may be granted salvation. The Reformed Churches thus adopted a belief in predestination and the enslavement of the will by the flesh for those not predestined to salvation.

The Reformation, which began in Germany and spread quickly throughout Europe, was a reaction to the corruption and administrative abuse in the Church. It expressed an alternate view of Christianity in practice and led to the creation and rise of Protestantism, with all its individual branches.

The movement grew in popularity, especially in Northern Europe, though reaction to the protests against the church varied from country to country. In 1529, the Holy Roman Emperor Charles V tried to stop the dissension among German Catholics. Elector John the Steadfast (1468–1532) was actively hostile to the emperor and one of the fiercest defenders of Protestantism. By the middle of the century, most of North and West Germany had become Protestant. King Henry VIII of England, who had been a steadfast Catholic, broke with the church over the pope's refusal to annul his marriage to Catherine of Aragon, the first of Henry's six wives. With the Act of Supremacy in 1534, Henry was made head of the Church of England, a title that would be shared by all future kings. John Calvin's *Institutes of the Christian Religion* (1536) codified the doctrines of the new faith, becoming the basis for Presbyterianism. In the moderate camp, Desiderius Erasmus of Rotterdam (1466–1536), though an opponent of the Reformation, remained committed to the reconciliation of Catholics and Protestants, a goal that would be partially realized in 1555 with the Religious Peace of Augsburg, a ruling by the Diet of the Holy Roman Empire granting freedom of worship to Protestants.

Two distinct branches of Protestantism grew out of the Reformation. The evangelical churches in Germany and Scandinavia were followers of Martin Luther, and the reformed churches in other countries were followers of John Calvin and Huldreich Zwingli. A third significant branch, *episcopacy* (government by bishops), developed in England. Many Anglicans rejected the word *Protestant* because they tended to agree with Roman Catholicism on most doctrinal points, while rejecting the primacy of the pope, preferring the collective governance of bishops.

Congregationalism and Presbyterianism both developed a form of government by the congregation, and were considered a return to early Christianity's communal governance as described in the New Testament.

In the Protestant movement there was a tendency to minimize liturgy and to stress preaching by the ministry and the reading of the Bible. Although Protestants rejected asceticism and monasteries, they encouraged, in some cases required, an elevated standard of personal morality. In some sects, notably Puritanism, a high degree of austerity was also required.

The doctrine that the individual conscience is the valid interpreter of Scripture led to a wide variety of Protestant sects; this fragmentation was further extended by doctrinal disputes within the sects notably over grace, predestination, and the sacraments. Many new Protestant movements have claimed new revelations, notably the Church of Jesus Christ of Latter-Day Saints, commonly known as Mormons.

The many denominations in Protestantism include Adventists, Anabaptists, Baptists, Calvinism, Congregationalism, Lutheranism, Methodism, Pentecostalism, Presbyterianism, Puritanism, spiritism, and Unitarianism. Individual churches include the Brethren; Christian Catholic Church; Disciples of Christ; Christian Reformed Church; Church of Jesus Christ of Latter-Day Saints; Church of the New Jerusalem; Church of Christ; General Conference of the Churches of God; Evangelical and Reformed Church; Evangelical United Brethren Church; Religious Society of Friends (Quakers); Huguenots; Mennonites; Moravian Church; Ranters; Reformed Church in America; Salvation Army; Church of Scotland; Free Church of Scotland; Seventh-Day Baptists; Shakers; United Church of Canada; and Universalist Church of America.

A Broader View

THE ROMAN CATHOLIC REFORMATION

The Roman Catholic Church mounted a Reformation of its own – if one can call it that, since Martin Luther was himself a Catholic. As Pope Paul IV lay dying in August of 1559, he lamented to Father Laynez: "From the time of St. Peter there has not been a pontificate so unfortunate as mine. How I regret the past! Pray for me." It appeared to be a bad time for the Church. Luigi Mocenigo, a Venetian ambassador to Papacy, sent this report on the situation: "In many countries, obedience to the pope has almost ceased, and matters are becoming so critical that, if God does not interfere, they will soon be desperate. Germany leaves little hope of being cured. Poland is in almost as hopeless a state. The disorders which have just lately taken place in France and Spain are too well known for me to speak of them; and the Kingdom of England, after returning a short time since to her old obedience, has again fallen into heresy. Thus the spiritual power of the pope is so straitened that the only remedy is a council summoned by the common consent of all princes. Unless this reduces the affairs of religion to order, a grave calamity is to be feared."

The need for a Reformation was due to the many abuses in the lives of the clergy and the people. In the central offices of the Church, political interests and a worldly life had come to preoccupy their attention. Many bishops and abbots carried themselves as secular rulers rather than as servants of the Church, especially in countries where they were also territorial princes. Many members of cathedrals were chiefly concerned with their income and how to increase it, especially by uniting several stipends in the hands of one person, who thus enjoyed a larger income and greater power. Luxury prevailed widely among the higher clergy, while the lower clergy were often poor, oppressed, and despairing. The scientific and spiritual training of the clergy was so poor that it was not surprising that there was ignorance and abuse. The moral standard of the clergy was also astonishingly low. The condition of many of the monasteries for men and women (which were often homes for the unmarried daughters of the nobility) was deplorable. As a result, the former prestige of the clergy had declined and its members were often regarded with scorn. As to the Christian people themselves, in numerous districts ignorance, superstition, religious indifference, and immorality had become the way of life. Add to all of this the Church's selling of dispensations for the forgiveness of sins, which was a travesty of Jesus' teachings, and you have the need for dramatic reform.

With the election of Pope Pius IV in 1560, the Catholic Church began a Reformation of its own. In 1561, as Ambassador Mocenigo had recommended, "a council of all princes" met in Trent. Actually, the Council of Trent had begun meeting in 1537, but its meeting in 1561 was one of the most contentious and yet most important gatherings ever. Despite the many quarrels and divisions, the church leaders agreed on many things that needed to be changed. The council ultimately identified many reforms. An unexpected side benefit of this gathering was that the Catholic bishops and representatives of various countries came to know one another as never before. When they returned to their respective countries, they returned with a new sense of the unity of the Church and its genuine sensitivity to the changing needs of the people. They also shook off the weight of their former hesitancy to change and were ready for reform.

In contrast to this new unity within the leaders of the Catholic Church, the Protestants were growing in their disagreements and divisions. Nevertheless, the Catholic Church would never again be the sole Christian religious organization in Northern Europe and England.

Amazingly, in the very midst of these problems, the missionary efforts of the Catholic Church were succeeding as never before. Driven by Jesus' directive in Mark 13:10 that "the gospel must first be preached to all nations," the Church had a sense of mission and a strong missionary program. While war (The 30 Years' War and others), the Protestant movement, and the challenges of the Reformation hampered progress in Europe, the larger continents of America, Asia, and Africa offered new frontiers for the spiritual energy of many of the Church's devoted. Beginning with Francis Xavier, founder of the Jesuits, many spiritually inspired missionaries set out to spread the gospel. Antonio Criminale, Roberto de' Nobili, Ridolfo Acquaviva, Matteo Ricci, and Adam Schall journeyed into India and China. Padre Valignano traveled to Japan. Abyssinia and the Congo were evangelized by Fathers Nunez, Baretto, and Sylveira. There were dangerous and heroic struggles to introduce the gospel to the Indians in North and South America. In Central America, the Franciscan and Dominican friars and the secular clergy had labored long before the Jesuits. In 1622 the Catholic Church developed the Roman Congregation "De Propaganda Fide," with its organized missionaries to the world beyond Europe.

The results speak for themselves. Today the number of Catholic Christians has exceeded one billion baptized members, with nearly four million of these working in some capacity within the Church.

The Protestant Christians have also taken hold of Jesus' directive to spread the gospel to the world, building their own missionary structure and program. As a result, in a world of approximately a little over six billion people in the year 2000, a little over two billion are Christians. Of the remaining people, nearly one billion are defined as non-religious or declared atheists. The next largest religious population is Islam, with 1.2 billion members. If we consider the children of Abraham to be the Jews, Christians, and Muslims, then the world population of their religious descendants (not racial descendants) is three and a half billion. A little more than half of the world's population is associated with a religion (Judaism, Christianity, Islam) that began with the people who descended from Abraham, and the promise from God to multiply their seed "as the stars in heaven," Genesis 22:17.

THE ECUMENICAL MOVEMENT

On January 6, 1928, Pope Pius XI issued an Encyclical on Religious Unity. In it he wrote: "Never perhaps in the past have we seen, as we see in these our own times, the minds of men so occupied by the desire both of strengthening and of extending to the common welfare of human society that fraternal relationship which binds and unites us together, and which is a consequence of our common origin and nature. All who invoke the name of Christ should abstain from mutual reproaches and at long last be united in mutual charity." Pius XI went on to quote Jesus' admonition to his disciples in John 13:34-35: "A new commandment I give to you, that you love one another; even as I have loved you, that you also love one another. By this all men will know that you are my disciples, if you have love for one another."

Since the 1960s there have been new movements to reconcile the many Christian Churches, the Protestant Denominations with the Catholics and Eastern Orthodox (Greek, Russian, and Coptic). Even though the effort has proven more difficult than imagined, there have been major breakthroughs to new levels of respect, appreciation, and cooperation among the many divisions.

Today we have the World Council of Churches (WCC), World Evangelical Alliance (WEA), the previously unimagined unity between Catholics and Evangelical Christians in the Catholic-Evangelical Accord. We have

Beliefnet, The National Council of Churches, The World Council of Churches, Worldwide Faith News, World Alliance of Reformed Churches, Church World Service, Lutheran World Federation, Conference of European Churches, Ecumenical News International, Gospel Communication Network, Jewish Christian Relations, Interfaith Community Ministries Network, and National Association of Ecumenical and Interreligious Staff.

But there is a long way to go before a unified Christianity is realized, if that is even possible. Some Christians believe that the movement to unify is a subversive, Antichrist movement away from Truth. Uniting all Christians may seem to be a good work, but there's a feeling of faithlessness in believers with different approaches to salvation, compromising those approaches in order to get along with others who have different interpretations and methods. Instead of unifying, some just want to have a better spirit of mutual appreciation among the many variations of Christianity. In other words, we can love one another as Christ instructed and still have our unique views and practices.

A Broader View

Chapter Five
THE MYSTICAL, METAPHYSICAL MESSIAH-CHRIST

IN THE IMAGE OF GOD

Jesus' teaching that we are gods (John 10:34) within God is a difficult teaching to understand given our present state of consciousness. Yet there is much support for this idea in ancient legends and myths. Around the world human mythology contains tales of ancient gods. Hindus, Egyptians, Chinese, Pacific Islands people, Incas, Mayans, Aztecs, Hopi, Algonquins, Norsemen, Greeks, Romans, and many others have legends of these ancient gods. Many of the legends contain similar story lines: There was a time when powerful gods battled with one another and intermingled with humans. In the biblical Genesis there were two groups of beings on the Earth in ancient times: Sons of God and the sons and daughters of men. These two groups eventually mingled, producing a third group of beings called "Nephilim." The Nephilim were power giants, humans with godlike strength and size. The intermingling of gods with humans so upset God that he decided to destroy mankind and the Nephilim and start over. Genesis 6:1-7 tells the story: "And it came to pass, when men began to multiply on the face of the ground, and daughters were born unto them, that the sons of God saw the daughters of men that they were fair; and they took them wives of all that they chose. And Jehovah said, 'My spirit shall not strive with man for ever, for now he also is flesh; yet shall his days be a hundred and twenty years.' The Nephilim were in the earth in those days, and also after that, when God's sons came to men's daughters. They bore children to them. The same [the children of these matings] were the mighty men who were of old, men of renown. The Lord saw that the wickedness of man was great in the earth, and that every imagination of the thoughts of his heart was only evil continually. The Lord was sorry that he had made man on the earth, and it grieved him in his heart. The Lord said, 'I will destroy man whom I have created....'"

In Numbers 13:33 we have a scene in which some men came into the presence of these giants: "And there we saw the Nephilim, the sons of Anak, who come of the Nephilim. We were in our own sight as grasshoppers, and so we were in their sight." The Incas also have legends about these giants living in their South American lands in ancient times. They say that a full-grown Inca man was only as tall as the length of the lower legs of these giants, only up to their knees. The Incas also tell that these giants were evil, and God came and took them out of the world through death, and they were seen no more (for the whole Inca myth see *Ancient South America*, Little and Van Auken, 2002).

The creation story is present in the Bible, but few read it carefully enough to notice the layers of creation. In the Book of Genesis, God first creates humanity in his own image, after his likeness, which would certainly qualify us to be godlings of the Most High God, as the psalmist stated in Psalm 82. Let's review this story more carefully.

In the very first chapter of Genesis, written in the Hebrew, the word used for God is *Elohim*, a *plural* Hebrew word that may be interpreted as "the Deities," and the crucial verse, 1:26, is commonly translated, my emphasis: "Let *us* make man in *our* image, after *our* likeness." Actually, the word *man* is not an accurate translation, because the original text uses the Hebrew word *adam*, which when used with a lowercase "a" means humankind in the *collective* sense. In Numbers 31:28, 30, 35, 40, and 46 the word *adam* is translated by scholars as "persons," conveying the broader meaning for the word *adam*. In later chapters of Genesis, when the word *adam* is capitalized, it becomes a proper name for a specific person, perhaps even a specific group of persons. But in the first two chapters *adam* simply means *person* or *persons*. Therefore, the critical line may be translated: "Let us make persons in our image, after our likeness." We might call them human beings except for the fact that they were not created in physical form until Genesis 2:7, a point many miss. In Chapter One there is only the *essence* of heaven and earth; nothing on the physical earth is alive yet, not even humans, as Genesis 2:5 clearly states: "And no plant of the field was yet in the earth, and no herb of the field had yet sprung up; for the Lord God had not caused it to rain upon the earth and there was not a man to till the ground." The man or being had been created in Elohim's image in Chapter One but not yet in physical form and placed on the Earth. We were in the mind and spirit of God, our Maker, and our "form" was consciousness and spirit.

But before we go further, let's try to understand why the author of Genesis used a *plural* word for the name of the initial Creator. And why, then, does he change God's name as the biblical story progresses: *Elohim, Yahweh Elohim, Yahweh, Adoni,* and *Jehovah*? I believe the answer is not that there is a pantheon of gods but that the one God is not an individual entity separate from anything or anyone; all exists within this *collective* God. The "many" of creation exists in the collective Oneness of this Creator. Therefore, the plural word better reflects the collective nature of the ultimate, universal, infinite God of creation. God is not an individual, separate entity from the whole of creation. Rather, the creation exists within the infinite "body" and mind of this collective, creator God, this

Elohim. We may consider Elohim to be the vast, infinite, eternal womb of consciousness within which all life was conceived, the mind of God. The physical creation does not begin until later in Chapter Two of Genesis. And when this physical creation begins, God's name is changed to *Yahweh Elohim*, which most English Bibles translate as "Lord God." God is only *Yahweh* by chapter four; and as the Bible continues, God is called *Adoni* or *Adonay*, from a root word that means sovereign, lord, master, or owner. For much of the Old Testament, God's name is *Jehovah*. Eventually, Jesus calls God *Abba*, which most English Bibles translate as "Father," but Abba more closely correlates to the English word "Papa" than it does to Father. For Jesus, God was an intimate Creator comparable in relationship and love to one's earthly papa. *Papa* would also mean that we are indeed the children of God, and as such are certainly godlings of the parent God.

Changing the name of the Creator reflects changes in our relationship to our Creator as the creation progressed. Originally, we were created in God's image. We were part of the collective, the "great assembly" spoken of in Psalm 82. The nature of the collective, universal God, who is creator of the whole universe, is spirit and consciousness; therefore, our divine nature is spirit and consciousness.

As the creation continued, a new dimension was added to us in Chapter Two of Genesis, a dimension formed from the dust of the Earth by Yahweh Elohim. Our second nature is physical form. Thus we are now body, mind, and spirit. This has become our predominant condition today. After the Chapter-One creation in the image and likeness of Elohim, Chapter Two records the second creation this way:

"Yahweh Elohim [Lord God] formed adam [person, persons, humankind] from the dust of the ground, and breathed into his nostrils the breath of life; and adam became a living soul. Yahweh Elohim planted a garden

A Broader View

eastward, in Eden, and there he put the man [person or persons] whom he had formed."

Let me again explain that most English Bibles will translate the Hebrew word *adam* as "man." But *adam* also means, and is translated by many scholars as, "persons" or "beings." It is helpful to hold that meaning in these initial chapters because it better expresses characteristics of this creation that are significant as our understanding grows.

In this verse we discover that we were created a second time, but this time from the dust of the ground and the breath of life. Therefore, we have been created twice. This is the origin of the idea that we have a dual nature: divine and human, godly and physical, spirit and flesh, essence and form, energy and matter.

But there is even a third creation! In the eighteenth verse of Chapter Two, Yahweh Elohim decides that we are "lonely" in this new world of duality: "And the Lord God said, 'It is not good that the man [person or persons] should be alone; I will make a help meet for him.'" God's first attempt to provide us with a companion or help-meet is with the animal kingdom, but "the man" finds no companion or help-meet among the creatures. Therefore, Yahweh Elohim casts "a deep sleep" over the being [adam] and separates *ishshah* and *ish*, these Hebrew words literally meaning female and male. In doing this Yahweh Elohim creates new gender-specific bodies, one feminine and the other masculine. Now we have a third layer to our whole being. We are divinely in the image of Elohim, physically of the dust of the Earth, and subsequently gender separated!

But if we continue to read Genesis carefully, there is another creation yet to come. As the creation continues, it reaches that point that we have already discussed concerning the Nephilim, the increase of evil to such a level that God decides to destroy everything and start over. Post-Great-Flood beings were apparently different than

A Broader View

Pre-Great-Flood beings. One significant difference was the end of the ages of the sons of God and of the giant Nephilim. After the Great Flood, an event recorded in the legends of cultures around the world, the Earth was only populated by humans. The godlings were no longer in the physical realms. Even the great prophets, many of whom performed miracles, were very human. Now our human nature was predominant, our divine subordinate, subliminal.

A fascinating event that is pertinent to our topic occurs in the Book of Job. As you may know, this book begins, 1:6: "Now it happened on the day when the sons of God came to present themselves before Yahweh, that Satan also came among them." God asks Satan to consider how "perfect and upright" Job is and how he "turns away from evil." To this, Satan replies with the greatest accusations against us: "Does Job not fear you for a reason? You have blessed the work of his hands, and his substance is increased in the land. But put forth your hand now and touch all that he has, and he will curse you to your face." In other words, we don't honor God because we love our Creator but because we fear losing our material riches and comforts if we offend Him. It is our wealth and physical well-being that matters to us, not our loving, mutually considerate relationship with God. To this accusation God responds with a major directive that we should all take to heart. He instructs Satan to test Job to see if this is so. And, as we all know, Job endures the dreadful tests without cursing God. Eventually, Job attempts to explain God's reasons for allowing such to happen to him, but God comes to him directly. And it is in this discussion that we find something integrally pertinent to our discussion of Jesus' teaching that we are gods (John 10:34). Here's the passage from Job 38:17:

"Then Jehovah answered Job out of the whirlwind and said, 'Who is this that darkens counsel by words without knowledge? Now gird up your loins like a man. For I will ask you, and you instruct me! Where were you when I laid the foundations of the earth? Tell me, if you have understanding. Who set its measures, if you know? Or who stretched the line on it? On what were its foundations fastened? Or who laid its cornerstone, When the morning stars sang together, And all the sons of God shouted for joy?"

God is demanding that Job search his heart for deeper answers to some very strange questions. Where was Job when the foundations of the Earth were laid out? To Job and to each of us today, this is a strange question indeed. We feel so connected to physical life, how could we possibly have been anywhere when the foundations of the Earth were set! But we were. We were among the "morning stars that sang together" when "the sons of God shouted for joy." A godly part of us, made in the image of our Creator, was with God when He laid the foundations of the Earth.

Edgar Cayce, from his deep attunement to the Universal Consciousness, taught that not only God is God, but each of us is a part of that oneness (Cayce, 900-181). We need to awaken to our divinity and our role with our Creator. Then, we need to integrate this divine nature with our human nature in order to fully realize who we are and what life is really about.

Jesus actually addresses the need for a change from such a predominant human focus to a more spiritual, heavenly focus when he tells Nicodemus that we must be born again, explaining that the physical, fleshly part of us is not sufficient but must give birth to the spiritual portion of our being. In the course of teaching this, Jesus actually tells us through Nicodemus that no one ascends to heaven who did not already descend from it. Within us is a heavenly being, who knows heaven firsthand and has come into this world from heaven. This teaching is found in John 3:6-14:

"'That which is born of the flesh is flesh. That which is born of the Spirit is spirit. Do not marvel that I said to you, 'You must be born anew.' The wind blows where it wants to, and you hear its sound but don't know where it comes from and where it is going. So is everyone who is born of the Spirit.' Nicodemus answered him, 'How can these things be?' Jesus answered him, 'Are you a teacher of Israel, and don't understand these things? Most assuredly I tell you, we speak that which we know, and testify of that which we have seen, and you don't receive our witness. If I told you earthly things and you don't believe, how will you believe if I tell you heavenly things? No one has ascended into heaven, but he who descended out of heaven, even the Son of Man, who is in heaven.'"

Notice in this last sentence that Jesus, the Son of Man, states that even though he is physically standing before Nicodemus, he is already in heaven. This indicates that heaven is in some sense a state of consciousness and can be accessed at any time from anywhere if the mind and heart are attuned to or conscious of heaven's essence.

No one ascends to heaven but he or she who descended from it. That is, a part of us has already been in heaven and descended into our baby body upon physical birth. Most of us have lost touch with this part. It is like our spiritual, divine, godly self that we discussed in the first chapter of Genesis, but we've become so focused on the physical outer world and our fleshly self, that we've lost awareness of our spiritual, godly self.

Jesus gives a further insight into this in the Gospel of John 14:4-11, during his Last Supper discussions with Thomas and Philip. Here's the discussion: Jesus says, "'Where I go, you know the way.' Thomas says to him, 'Lord, we do not know where you go; how can we know the way?' Jesus says to him, 'I am the way, and the truth, and the life; no one comes to the Father, but by me. If you had known me, you would have known my Father also; from now on you know him, and have seen him.' Philip says to him, 'Lord, show us the Father, and it is sufficient for us.' Jesus says to him, 'Have I been with you this long a time, and you do not know me, Philip? He that has seen me has seen the Father; how can you say, 'Show us the Father?' Don't you believe that I am in the Father, and the Father is in me? The words that I say to you I speak not from myself, but the Father abiding in me does his works. Believe me that I am in the Father, and the Father in me; or else believe me for the very works' sake.'"

In this discussion we discover that somewhere deep within us, we know where Jesus went and we know the way! How? Because, as he taught Nicodemus, not one of us ascends to heaven that did not already descend from it, and deep within us we have known heaven and we know the way to heaven. But, like most of us, Philip wants Jesus to manifest the Father out here in the physical, outer world, where we predominantly live and have our being. However, Jesus redirects him toward the Father's realm, as found in that teaching he gave in Luke 17:22: "The kingdom of God is within you." Jesus explains that if you see and know me, you see and know the Father because "I am in the Father, and the Father is in me." But these are hard words to accept when living predominantly in an externalized, outwardly projected state of consciousness. Inner places and spaces are not our common abode for consciousness and activity. Prayer, meditation, dreams, intuition, inner listening to our deeper self, and inner listening to God's "still, small voice" within us are all ways to find the way, the truth, and the light as Jesus exemplified it.

CHILDREN OF GOD

One of the many amazing discourses that came through Edgar Cayce's attunement to the Universal Consciousness begins with a series of driving questions. And he would not let anyone pull away until the answers and the profound implications of these answers were fully realized. Here are the questions: "Are you not all children of God? Are you not co-creators with Him? Have you not been with Him from the beginning? Is there any knowledge, wisdom or understanding withheld if you have attuned yourself to that Creative Force which made the worlds and all the forces manifested in same? Do you think that the arm of God is ever short with you because you have erred? 'Though you be afar, though you be in the uttermost parts, if you call I will *hear!* and answer speedily.' Do you think that is spoken to another, or to you?" (Cayce, 294-202)

Hard for us to wiggle our way out of accepting his line of thought. Yet we may certainly ask ourselves, If this is true, what has happened to us? We are becoming increasingly aware that our little Earth is only a speck, only a dot in a universe of worlds. And each of us is but one person among billions. Why and how is God mindful of a little individual among billions on an insignificant dot in a vast universe of worlds? Cayce gives this answer: "SPIRIT! For our spirit is a portion of His Spirit, and ever bears witness with His Spirit as to whether we be the children of God or not." (Cayce, 262-115) The enormity of the universe exists within God's infinite Spirit, and each of us was given, was made with, a portion of that Spirit. Therefore, wherever we are, however many other souls there are, each and every one of us has a portion of the Spirit of God within us. And this is why and how God is mindful of each one of us. Cayce said, "Know that not only

God is God, but *self* is a part of that Oneness." (Cayce, 900-181)

"You are indeed the children of God. And as children in your Wisdom you may approach boldly the Throne of Mercy. For the prayers of the righteous are heard, for they have attuned in Wisdom to the God-Consciousness within. Then make your paths straight. Let your conversation, your wishes, your desires be rather as one with Him who thought it not robbery to be equal with God." (Cayce, 262-105)

It is difficult to consider ourselves equal with God – actual offspring and companions to the Creator of this infinite universe. There are, according to several Cayce readings, three key reasons for our doubts: (1) We don't make enough room in our lives, in our conversations, in our thinking for our better selves to come through; (2) We block God's mercy, understanding, and forgiveness; mostly through judgments and condemnations against ourselves and others; and (3) We cling to self-seeking interests and material gratifications, budgeting little time for God-consciousness.

How have we gotten so far away from the truth about our divinity? Cayce's discourses explain that it began a very long time ago, long before Earth, when the children of God began using their God-given free wills in ways that were neither compatible with the Creative Spirit nor in harmony with Life's unfolding plan. He explains that that which is sown with free will grows and blossoms, and its fruit reflects the intention and "motivative forces" with which it was sown. Therefore, seeds sown thoughtlessly produce the fruits of confusion and doubt. Seeds sown selfishly produce the fruits of greed, envy, jealousy, even hate, and are the seeds of loneliness and self-condemnation. However, the law of sow-and-reap is *always* in effect. Therefore, if we sow the very next seed *mindfully* and with the motivation to love, to be patient, and cooperative, then the fruits of our harvest will turn to good.

In a subtle but significant lesson, Cayce's readings teach us that we can only *sow* the good seeds and *cultivate* them. Beyond this, we must *leave* the magic of life and growth in God's hands. "God gives the increase," Cayce instructs. Our role is to sow and cultivate well, leaving the outcome to the Creative Forces, (Cayce, 262-115). Too often we attempt to tell God how best to manifest the results, and in doing so, we often limit God's gifts to us and to those we love.

Cayce's readings also tell us that we are not alone in our efforts to reawaken to our full potential. We have a "bridge" or "intermediary" to God that we can access during our days here. It is the Christ Spirit. Unfortunately, some humans have damaged the image and truth about Jesus Christ and his role in human spirituality. They have damaged his loving mercy ("Forgive seventy times seven," Matthew 18:20, and "Neither do I condemn you; go your way and sin no more," John 8:11) by making him out to be a letter-of-the-law person. They have damaged his openness to all ("He that is not against us is for us," Mark 9:40, and "Other sheep I have which are not of this fold." John 10:16) by making him out to be a judge and condemner of all who do not call upon his name. And they have damaged his understanding of humanity ("The spirit is indeed willing, but the flesh is weak," Matthew 26:41) by making him out to be above humanity, even though he, too, was tempted and tested by evil and declared himself to be our friend, our brother, in the struggles of life.

Unfortunately, the public sins of the Christian Church have also overshadowed the good in Christian concepts and ways.

Nevertheless, Cayce's readings don't pull away from the truth about Christ, a truth far bigger than Christianity has understood. From Cayce's perspective, "Christ is not a man. Jesus was the man; Christ the messenger; Christ in all ages, Jesus in one." (Cayce, 991-1) For Cayce, Christ is a global Spirit of God's presence with us, with *all* of us. And this Spirit is accessible to all, no matter where they live or what they have been raised on. He equates Christ with "love of God-consciousness." (Cayce, 281-13) From Cayce's perspective, the Christ Spirit, as manifested through Jesus, is a powerful resource for the children of God to call upon in their quest to regain awareness of God and their personal spirituality. "As He has given, 'If you love me, keep my commandments; for they are not grievous to bear. For I will bear them *with* you, I will wipe away your tears; I will comfort the brokenhearted, I will bring all in the Wisdom of God for your expressions through each experience, in each activity of yours.' You know the way. Let, then, that love of the Infinite fire you to action, to *doing*! And indeed live as has been shown." (Cayce, 262-105)

As Jesus was leaving to be at-one with God again, he spoke of this Spirit, "I will not leave you comfortless.... But the Comforter, the Holy Spirit, whom the Father will send in my name, he shall teach you all things, and bring to your remembrance all that I said to you.... When he, the Spirit of truth, is come, he shall guide you in all the truth; for he shall not speak from himself; but whatsoever he shall hear [from God], these shall he speak; and he shall declare to you the things that are to come." (excerpts from John 14-16)

Cayce's readings ask us: "Will you each as individuals be led by the Spirit of Truth? Or will self, your own ego, your material desire, so outweigh that purpose, that hope, that mission for which each soul is given the opportunity in material expression? Here we find much that may need analyzing, looking into, in our own individual experiences. Do we, as children of God, as seekers after God, have *firsthand* knowledge? Or do we accept only that others have told us? Do we *know*, or is it only self-righteousness that speaks? Are we *living* that life? Let each ask self, 'do I manifest – in speech, in activity – that I sincerely believe? Do I give credit to the spirit where credit is due? Do I adhere to the spirit of brotherly love? Do I sow the seeds of kindness with a kindly feeling, or with merely a sense of duty? Do I have long-suffering because I just can't help myself, or because I am willing that God through His Son, through the Master of masters, show me the way?'" (Cayce, 262-125)

One of Cayce's regular requests was that we learn how to become consciously aware of God's presence and promptings within us. How can we lay aside the physical self in order for the Spirit and Mind of our Maker to guide and renew us? The first way is natural. We all sleep. And Cayce teaches that when we are "absent from the body," we are "present in the Spirit." To enter sleep mindfully and with the intention of meeting the Spirit-Mind of God is to sow and cultivate the seed of enlightenment. Throughout the Bible we are told of seekers who experienced God and God's guidance in dreams. In Job 33:14-17, we find this marvelous but often overlooked teaching: "For God speaks once, and twice, though man pays no attention. In a dream, in a vision of the night, when deep sleep falls on men, in slumbering on the bed; then he opens the ears of men, and seals their instruction, that he may withdraw man from his [self-centered] purpose, and hide pride from man. He keeps back his soul from the pit." Dreams are a valuable means for heavenly guidance and insight. Not all dreams. Dreams and interpreting dreams are difficult. The language of the deeper consciousness is no longer familiar to us. But when one regularly practices remembering and interpreting dreams, then one awakens to one's potential for deep, heavenly communication.

The second way is not as natural as dreaming. It is through conscious intention to set aside our outer minds and concerns in daily moments of prayer and meditation.

These moments open our minds and hearts to the inner Spirit-Mind. It is difficult to still the outer mind, but as God instructed in Psalm 46:11: "Be still, and know that I am God." In the stillness comes the Presence of God and God's blessing. As Elijah explained in 1 Kings 19:12, he searched for God in all the powerful forces of Earth – lightning, earthquakes, wind, and fire – but found God's presence in a "still, small voice" within.

And the third way is to speak, think, and act as if God were consciously with us in our daily activity. Practicing the *presence* of God is a golden way to transform our lives and the lives of those around us – if, of course, it is done in love, patience, and cooperation rather than judgment and condemnation of others and oneself.

Each of us needs to gain his or her own direct, personal contact with our Maker. "Who knows better than the individuals themselves what has hindered them from being physically, mentally, spiritually in accord with the divine that is life manifested in the body? From whence comes that individual entity's ability to cope with the problems?" (Cayce, 294-202) Obviously, the answer to this last question is that it only comes from within the individuals themselves. Doctors have said often that much of the recovery of physical illness is determined from somewhere within the person. This reading is saying that it is from God within, from the individual's own Maker.

"God seeks all to be one with Him. And as all things were made by Him, that which is the creative influence in every herb, mineral, vegetable, or individual activity is that same force you call God, and *seeks* expression!" (Cayce, 294-202)

Let's accept that we are the children of God and reflect that in our thoughts and actions. Such a change in our identity is likely to transform us more than all the other concepts and practices.

CHRIST CONSCIOUSNESS

Edgar Cayce gave 181 readings on the topic of Christ Consciousness. In one of them (Cayce, 272-9) he teaches that we are all born with desires, abilities, weaknesses, and strengths, and find ourselves subject to hereditary influences that give our bodies strengths and weaknesses. We also find ourselves in circumstances and relationships that appear to challenge our weaknesses and demand our strengths. In the midst of all of this, Cayce reminds us that those who seek God, the heavenly Father-Mother, the Creative Forces, will find that a way of escape from those things that so easily beset us is prepared, if we will but become more one with our Creator and God's will. But each of us must voluntarily choose "the Way." Nothing, no weakness or desire, no circumstance or gene, is more powerful than our will, our free will, given as a gift from God. But we must choose to engage it, selecting that which is right, is just, is sincere, is honest in our activities with ourselves and others.

Paradoxically, the way of escape from those things that beset us is not outside of us (a rich uncle, a new medical technique, a better companion, more money, and so on) but is *within* us. Cayce teaches: "The way is simple. Yet those who would seek through the mysteries of nature, the mysteries of the manifestations of life in the earth, or those who would see [and follow] the activities of their neighbors, friends, associates, [rather] than listen to that which may be had through the still small voice from within, become in the position of being troubled and wondering – and then fearful; and then there come those periods when the sureness of self is lacking." All healing, wisdom, soul growth, and true love comes from within us, from our oneness with the Spirit that gives life to all the transcending powers that lift us to higher levels of love, joy, peace, and contentment.

Christ-consciousness is a growing *inner* awareness of our personal connection with God and the Creative Forces, as subtle and gentle as they may be. The biblical instruction is to first "seek the kingdom of God and all else will be given to you." (Matthew 6:33 and Luke 12:31) This inner connection, this consciousness, is the way.

FRUITS OF THE SPIRIT

Daily life provides many opportunities to apply this growing awareness of God with us in our actions, words, and thoughts. As we strive to include God in our lives and relationships, our work and our play, we become imbued with God's *presence*, God's *consciousness*. We become God conscious, which awakens the godliness within our deeper nature. Applying the fruits of the Spirit in our lives results in us becoming increasingly one with the Spirit. According to Paul, in Galatians 5:22-23, these are the fruits of the Spirit: love, joy, peace, long-suffering, gentleness, goodness, faith, meekness, and temperance. Cayce adds patience, mercy, kindness, and forgiveness. In Cayce's reading 1336-1, he explains: "Only in the fruits of the spirit may the *true meaning* of life's experience and the purposes of life ... be understood ... as a practical application ... in thy daily life with thy daily experience with thy fellow man." Applying the fruits of the Spirit in our daily lives spiritualizes our physical body and life and enhances our spiritual consciousness.

Jesus explained it this way: "In this is my Father glorified, that you bear much fruit; and so you will be my disciples. Even as the Father has loved me, I also have loved you. Remain in my love. If you keep my commandments, you will remain in my love; even as I have kept my Father's commandments, and remain in his love. I have spoken these things to you, that my joy may remain in you, and that your joy may be made full. This is my commandment, that you love one another, even as I have loved you." (John 15:8-12)

Throughout the Bible, love is most important. From Genesis to the Revelation, the Bible indicates that love evokes the highest, most godly of powers, and reflects the true nature of God, our Creator. We were conceived in God's love. The motivation for God to create us was an expression of love. Love, therefore, brings us closest to our true, divine nature – our angelic nature. Many biblical passages teach that of all the things a person can learn and do in this world, nothing reflects Godliness more than love. The two greatest commandments are found in both the Old and New Testaments. The first commandment is found in Deuteronomy 6:5 and Matthew 22:37:

"You shall love the Lord your God with all your heart, and with all your soul, and with all your mind."

The second commandment is found in Leviticus 19:18 and Matthew 22:39:

"You shall love your neighbor [*plesion*, meaning a 'close-by person'] as yourself."

The disciple Paul's famous love statement is found in 1 Corinthians 13:13: "Now abide faith, hope, and love, these three; but the greatest of these is love." Paul goes on to beautifully describe love: "Love is patient, love is kind, and is not jealous; love does not brag and is not arrogant, does not act unbecomingly; it does not seek its own, is not provoked, does not take into account a wrong suffered, does not rejoice in unrighteousness, but rejoices with the truth; bears all things, believes all things, hopes all things, endures all things. Love never fails."

Peter's love advice is in 1 Peter 4:8: "Above all things, keep fervent in your love for one another, because love covers a multitude of sins."

The disciple John gives his perspective in his letter, 1 John 4:7-12: "Beloved, let us love one another, for love is from God; and everyone who loves is born of God and knows God. The one who does not love does not know God, for God is love .... If we love one another, God abides in us, and His love is perfected in us."

Of all the fruits of the Spirit, love is the most important spirit with which to live daily life. Going through a day in the spirit of love imbues us with the Spirit of God. In lovingness, we regain our oneness with our Maker. "Love one another" is the new commandment, the new way. It is the best way to become conscious of the Messiah-Christ.

Now today we counter this with a concept of "tough love," meaning that the better love does not hide its head in the sand and overlook truth! Jesus was never a doormat. When it was necessary, he called others' attention to what they were doing and how they were affecting God's way, God plan. One good example is when he had just finished complimenting Peter on his wisdom and inner guidance (Matthew 16:17-19), and Peter then tried to keep him from going into Jerusalem to meet his destiny. Jesus turned again and said to Peter (Matthew 16:23): "Get behind me, Satan! You are a stumbling-block to me, for you are not setting your mind on the things of God, but on the things of men." Truth with love is the best course – truth, not judgment or condemnation, which should be left with God.

The Book of the Revelation predicts that a new era is coming, an era in which Satan will be bound for a period like unto a thousand years (Revelation 20:2). During this wonderful time there will be no evil. Love, the Spirit of God, will abound. Only those who have lived love and loved beyond all selfishness will be able to enjoy those times. It would be good to put it in our hearts to be part of those wonderful days. Ultimately, God is love. If we wish to be one with our Maker, then we are required to catch the spirit of love and make it a part of our spirit, our thinking. In some respects, God consciousness is loving consciousness. The message of the Messiah-Christ is a message of love, a call to love.

An excellent insight into this occurs during a discussion between Jesus and one of the scribes at the Temple in Jerusalem. It is found in Mark 12:28-34:
One of the scribes came, and heard them questioning together. Knowing that he [Jesus] had answered them well, asked him, "Which commandment is the greatest of all?" Jesus answered, "The greatest is, 'Hear, Israel, the Lord our God, the Lord is one: you shall love the Lord your God with all your heart, and with all your soul, and with all your mind, and with all your strength.' This is the first commandment. The second is like this, 'You shall love your neighbor as yourself.' There is no other commandment greater than these." The scribe said to him, "Truly, teacher, you have said well that He is one, and there is none other but He, and to love Him with all the heart, and with all the understanding, with all the soul, and with all the strength, and to love his neighbor as himself, is more important than all the whole burnt offerings and sacrifices." When Jesus saw that he answered wisely, he said to him, "You are not far from the Kingdom of God."

Conscious awareness of love, especially love for God and others, indeed brings us very close to the Kingdom of God.

A Broader View

Chapter Six
THE LIFE OF SAINT ISSA
Transcribed from Tibetan Texts
by Nicolas Notovitch

Nicolas Notovitch traveled throughout India, Tibet, and Afghanistan in the 1880s and wrote that while he was recovering from an injury at the Buddhist monastery Himis, in Ledak (then in the Western region of Tibet but today is in the northernmost part of India), he was shown a copy of a manuscript titled *The Life of Saint Issa*. Notovitch came to understand that *Issa* was a Buddhist equivalent of the name *Jesus*. He was told that the manuscript was about a "saint" from the West who had been revered by Hindus and Buddhists. He managed to have the manuscript read to him aloud, in translation, of course. To his amazement, it contained the whole story of Jesus' life, from twelve years of age until thirty. Notovitch said that the monks told him that the original of this copy was located in the monastery on Mt. Marbour, near Lhasa, with other copies at several of the country's other major monasteries. Notovitch published his book in 1894, *The Unknown Life of Jesus Christ*. Here is the text of this story.

CHAPTER I

1 The earth has trembled and the heavens have wept because of a great crime which has been committed in the land of Israel.

2 For they have tortured and there put to death the great and just Issa, in whom dwelt the soul of the universe,
3 Which was incarnate in a simple mortal in order to do good to men and to exterminate their evil thoughts
4 And in order to bring back man degraded by his sins to a life of peace, love, and happiness and to recall to him the one and indivisible Creator, whose mercy is infinite and without bounds.
5 Hear what the merchants from Israel relate to us on this subject.

CHAPTER II
1 The people of Israel, who dwelt on a fertile soil giving forth two crops a year and who possessed large flocks, excited by their sins the anger of God
2 Who inflicted upon them a terrible chastisement in taking from them their land, their cattle, and their possessions. Israel was reduced to slavery by the powerful and rich pharaohs who then reigned in Egypt.
3 These treated the Israelites worse than animals, burdening them with difficult tasks and loading them with chains. They covered their bodies with weals and wounds, without giving them food or permitting them to dwell beneath a roof,
4 To keep them in a state of continual terror and to deprive them of all human resemblance.
5 And in their great calamity, the people of Israel remembered their heavenly protector and, addressing themselves to him, implored his grace and mercy.
6 An illustrious pharaoh then reigned in Egypt who had rendered himself famous by his numerous victories, the riches he had heaped up, and the vast palaces which his slaves had erected for him with their own hands.
7 This pharaoh had two sons, of whom the younger was called Mossa. Learned Israelites taught him diverse sciences.

8 And they loved Mossa in Egypt for his goodness and the compassion which he showed to all those who suffered.

9 Seeing that the Israelites would not, in spite of the intolerable sufferings they were enduring, abandon their God to worship those made by the hand of man, which were gods of the Egyptian nation,

10 Mossa believed in their invisible God, who did not let their failing strength give way.

11 And the Israelitish preceptors excited the ardor of Mossa and had recourse to him, praying him to intercede with the pharaoh his father in favor of their co-religionists.

12 Wherefore the Prince Mossa went to his father, begging him to ameliorate the fate of these unfortunates. But the pharaoh became angered against him and only augmented the torments endured by his slaves.

13 It happened that a short time after, a great evil visited Egypt. The pestilence came to decimate there both the young and the old, the weak and the strong; and the pharaoh believed in the resentment of his own gods against him.

14 But the Prince Mossa told his father that it was the God of his slaves who was interceding in favor of these unfortunates in punishing the Egyptians.

15 The pharaoh then gave to Mossa his son an order to take all the slaves of the Jewish race, to conduct them outside the town, and to found at a great distance from the capital another city where he should dwell with them.

16 Mossa then made known to the Hebrew slaves that he had set them free in the name of their God, the God of Israel, and he went out with them from the city and from the land of Egypt.

17 He led them into the land they had lost by their many sins, he gave unto them laws, and enjoined them to pray always to the invisible Creator whose goodness is infinite.

18 On the death of Prince Mossa, the Israelites rigorously observed his laws, wherefore God recompensed them for the ills to which he had exposed them in Egypt.

19 Their kingdom became the most powerful of all the earth, their kings made themselves famous for their treasures, and a long peace reigned among the people of Israel.

CHAPTER III

1 The glory of the riches of Israel spread throughout the earth, and the neighboring nations bore them envy.

2 For the Most High himself led the victorious arms of the Hebrews, and the pagans dared not attack them.

3 Unhappily, as man is not always true to himself, the fidelity of the Israelites to their God did not last long.

4 They began by forgetting all the favors which he had heaped upon them, invoked but seldom his name, and sought the protection of magicians and sorcerers.

5 The kings and the captains substituted their own laws for those which Mossa had written down for them. The temple of God and the practice of worship were abandoned. The people gave themselves up to pleasure and lost their original purity.

6 Several centuries had elapsed since their departure from Egypt when God determined to exercise once more his chastisements upon them.

7 Strangers began to invade the land of Israel, devastating the country, ruining the villages, and carrying the inhabitants into captivity.

8 And there came at one time pagans from the country of Romeles, on the other side of the sea. They subdued the Hebrews and established among them military leaders who by delegation from Caesar ruled over them.

9 They destroyed the temples, they forced the inhabitants to cease worshipping the invisible God, and compelled them to sacrifice victims to the pagan deities.

10 They made warriors of those who had been nobles, the women were torn away from their husbands, and the lower classes, reduced to slavery, were sent by thousands beyond the seas.

11 As to the children, they were put to the sword. Soon in all the land of Israel naught was heard but groans and lamentations.

12 In this extreme distress, the people remembered their great God. They implored his grace and besought him to forgive them; and our Father, in his inexhaustible mercy, heard their prayer.

CHAPTER IV

1 At this time came the moment when the all-merciful Judge elected to become incarnate in a human being.

2 And the Eternal Spirit, dwelling in a state of complete inaction and of supreme beatitude, awoke and detached itself for an indefinite period from the Eternal Being,

3 So as to show forth in the guise of humanity the means of self-identification with Divinity and of attaining to eternal felicity,

4 And to demonstrate by example how man may attain moral purity and, by separating his soul from its mortal coil, the degree of perfection necessary to enter into the kingdom of heaven, which is unchangeable and where happiness reigns eternal.

5 Soon after, a marvelous child was born in the land of Israel, God himself speaking by the mouth of this infant of the frailty of the body and the grandeur of the soul.

6 The parents of the newborn child were poor people, belonging by birth to a family of noted piety, who, forgetting their ancient grandeur on earth, praised the name of the Creator and thanked him for the ills with which he saw fit to prove them.

7 To reward them for not turning aside from the way of truth, God blessed the firstborn of this family. He chose

him for his elect and sent him to help those who had fallen into evil and to cure those who suffered.

8 The divine child, to whom was given the name of Issa, began from his earliest years to speak of the one and indivisible God, exhorting the souls of those gone astray to repentance and the purification of the sins of which they were culpable.

9 People came from all parts to hear him, and they marveled at the discourses proceeding from his childish mouth. All the Israelites were of one accord in saying that the Eternal Spirit dwelt in this child.

10 When Issa had attained the age of thirteen years, the epoch when an Israelite should take a wife,

11 The house where his parents earned their living by carrying on a modest trade began to be a place of meeting for rich and noble people, desirous of having for a son-in-law the young Issa, already famous for his edifying discourses in the name of the Almighty.

12 Then it was that Issa left the parental house in secret, departed from Jerusalem, and with the merchants set out towards Sind,

13 With the object of perfecting himself in the Divine Word and of studying the laws of the great Buddhas.

CHAPTER V

1 In the course of his fourteenth year, the young Issa, blessed of God, came on this side of Sind and established himself among the Aryas in the land beloved of God.

2 Fame spread the reputation of this marvelous child throughout the length of northern Sind, and when he crossed the country of the five rivers and the Rajputana, the devotees of the god Jaine prayed him to dwell among them.

3 But he left the erring worshippers of Jaine and went to Juggernaut in the country of Orissa, where repose the

A Broader View

mortal remains of Vyasa-Krishna and where the white priests of Brahma made him a Joyous welcome.

4 They taught him to read and understand the Vedas, to cure by aid of prayer, to teach, to explain the holy scriptures to the people, and to drive out evil spirits from the bodies of men, restoring unto them their sanity.

5 He passed six years at Juggernaut, at Rajagriha, at Benares, and in the other holy cities. Everyone loved him, for Issa lived in peace with the Vaisyas and the Sudras, whom he instructed in the holy scriptures.

6 But the Brahmans and the Kshatriyas told him that they were forbidden by the great Para-Brahma to come near to those whom he had created from his side and his feet;

7 That the Vaisyas were only authorized to hear the reading of the Vedas, and this on festival days only;

8 That the Sudras were forbidden not only to assist at the reading of the Vedas, but also from contemplating them, for their condition was to serve in perpetuity as slaves to the Brahmans, the Kshatriyas, and even the Vaisyas.

9 "'Death only can set them free from their servitude' has said Para-Brahma. Leave them then and come and worship with us the gods, who will become incensed against thee if thou cost disobey them."

10 But Issa listened not to their discourses and betook him to the Sudras, preaching against the Brahmans and the Kshatriyas.

11 He inveighed against the act of a man arrogating to himself the power to deprive his fellow beings of their rights of humanity; "for," said he, "God the Father makes no difference between his children; all to him are equally dear."

12 Issa denied the divine origin of the Vedas* and the Puranas*. "For," taught he to his followers, "a law has already been given to man to guide him in his actions;
[The Abhedananda version of the Himis transcript does not include this denunciation]

13 "Fear thy God, bend the knee before him only, and bring to him alone the offerings which proceed from thy gains."

14 Issa denied the Trimurti and the incarnation of Para-Brahma in Vishnu, Siva*, and other gods, for said he: *[The Abhedananda version of the Himis transcript does not include this denunciation]

15 "The Judge Eternal, the Eternal Spirit, comprehends the one and indivisible soul of the universe, which alone creates, contains, and vivifies all. *Inasmuch as Jesus' closest disciple, John, begins his Gospel with a quote from the Vedas, "In the beginning was the Word . . . ," the authenticity of this passage may be questioned. (Notation added by Notovitch)

16 "He alone has willed and created, he alone has existed since all eternity, and his existence will have no end. He has no equal either in the heavens or on earth.

17 "The Great Creator has not shared his power with any living being, still less with inanimate objects, as they have taught to you; for he alone possesses omnipotence.

18 "He willed it and the world appeared. In a divine thought, he gathered together the waters, separating from them the dry portion of the globe. He is the principle of the mysterious existence of man, in whom he has breathed a part of his Being.

19 "And he has subordinated to man the earth, the waters, the beasts, and all that he has created and that he himself preserves in immutable order, fixing for each thing the length of its duration.

20 "The anger of God will soon be let loose against man; for he has forgotten his Creator, he has filled his temples with abominations, and he worships a crowd of creatures which God has made subordinate to him.

21 "For to do honor to stones and metals, he sacrifices human beings, in whom dwells a part of the spirit of the Most High.

22 "For he humiliates those who work by the sweat of their brow to acquire the favor of an idler seated at his sumptuous board.

23 "Those who deprive their brethren of divine happiness shall be deprived of it themselves. The Brahmans and the Kshatriyas shall become the Sudras, and with the Sudras the Eternal shall dwell everlastingly.
24 "Because in the day of the last judgment the Sudras and the Vaisyas will be forgiven much because of their ignorance, while God, on the contrary, will punish with his wrath those who have arrogated to themselves his rights."
25 The Vaisyas and the Sudras were filled with great admiration and asked Issa how they should pray so as not to lose their eternal felicity.
26 "Worship not the idols, for they hear you not. Listen not to the Vedas, for their truth is counterfeit. Never put yourself in the first place and never humiliate your neighbor.
27 "Help the poor, support the weak, do ill to no one, and covet not that which thou hast not and which thou seest belongeth to another."

*Sir John Wodroofe notes: "The fourth Gospel opens grandly, 'In the beginning was the Word, and the Word was with God and the Word was God.' These are the very words of Veda. *Prajapatir vai idam asit:* In the beginning was Brahman. *Tasya vag dvitya asit;* with whom was the Vak or the Word... *Vag vai paramam Brahma;* and the word is Brahman" (The Garland Letters, 7th ed. [Pondicherry: Ganesh & Co., 1979] p.4)

CHAPTER VI
1 The white priests and the warriors, becoming acquainted with the discourses of Issa addressed to the

Sudras, resolved upon his death and sent with this intent their servants to seek out the young prophet.

2 But Issa, warned of his danger by the Sudras, left the neighborhood of Juggernaut by night, reached the mountain, and established himself in the country of Gautamides, the birthplace of the great Buddha Sakyamuni, in the midst of a people worshipping the one and sublime Brahma.

3 After having perfected himself in the Pali language, the just Issa applied himself to the study of the sacred writings of the Sutras.

4 Six years after, Issa, whom the Buddha had elected to spread his holy word, had become a perfect expositor of the sacred writings.

5 Then he left Nepal and the Himalayan mountains, descended into the valley of Rajputana, and went towards the west, preaching to diverse peoples the supreme perfection of man,

6 Which is-to do good to one's neighbor, being the sure means of merging oneself rapidly in the Eternal Spirit: "He who shall have regained his original purity," said Issa, "will die having obtained remission for his sins, and he will have the right to contemplate the majesty of God."

7 In crossing pagan territories, the divine Issa taught that the worship of visible gods was contrary to the law of nature.

8 "For man," said he, "has not been permitted to see the image of God, and yet he has made a host of deities in the likeness of the Eternal.

9 "Moreover, it is incompatible with the human conscience to make less matter of the grandeur of divine purity than of animals and objects executed by the hand of man in stone or metal.

10 "The Eternal Lawgiver is one; there is no other God but he. He has not shared the world with anyone, neither has he informed anyone of his intentions.

11 "Even as a father would act towards his children, so will God judge men after their deaths according to the laws of his mercy. Never would he so humiliate his child as to transmigrate his soul, as in a purgatory, into the body of an animal."

12 "The heavenly law," said the Creator by the mouth of Issa, "is opposed to the immolation of human sacrifices to an image or to an animal; for I have consecrated to man all the animals and all that the earth contains.

13 "All things have been sacrificed to man, who is directly and intimately associated with me his Father; therefore he who shall have stolen from me my child will be severely judged and chastised by the divine law.

14 "Man is naught before the Eternal Judge, as the animal is naught before man.

15 "Wherefore I say unto you, Leave your idols and perform not rites which separate you from your Father, associating you with the priests from whom the heavens have turned away.

16 "For it is they who have led you from the true God and whose superstitions and cruelties conduce to the perversion of your soul and the loss of all moral sense."

CHAPTER VII

1 The words of Issa spread among the pagans in the midst of the countries he traversed, and the inhabitants forsook their idols.

2 Seeing which the priests exacted of him who glorified the name of the true God, reason in the presence of the people for the reproaches he made against them and a demonstration of the nothingness of their idols.

3 And Issa made answer to them: "If your idols and your animals are powerful and really possessed of supernatural strength, then let them strike me to the earth."

4 "Work then a miracle," replied the priests, "and let thy God confound our gods, if they inspire him with contempt."

5 But Issa then said: "The miracles of our God have been worked since the first day when the universe was created; they take place every day and at every moment. Whosoever seeth them not is deprived of one of the fairest gifts of life.

6 "And it is not against pieces of stone, metal, or wood, which are inanimate, that the anger of God will have full course; but it will fall on men, who, if they desire their salvation, must destroy all the idols they have made.

7 "Even as a stone and a grain of sand, naught as they are in the sight of man, wait patiently the moment when he shall take and make use of them,

8 "So man must await the great favor that God shall accord him in his final judgment.

9 "But woe unto you, ye enemies of men, if it be not a favor that you await but rather the wrath of the Divinity-woe unto you if ye expect miracles to bear witness to his power.

10 "For it will not be the idols that he will annihilate in his anger but those who shall have erected them. Their hearts shall be consumed with eternal fire, and their lacerated bodies shall go to satiate the hunger of wild beasts.

11 "God will drive the impure from among his flocks, but he will take back to himself those who shall have gone astray through not having recognized the portion of spirituality within them."

12 Seeing the powerlessness of their priests, the pagans had still greater faith in the sayings of Issa and, fearing the anger of the Divinity, broke their idols to pieces. As for the priests, they fled to escape the vengeance of the populace.

13 And Issa further taught the pagans not to strive to see the Eternal Spirit with their eyes but to endeavor to feel him in their hearts and by purity of soul to render themselves worthy of his favors.

14 "Not only," said he unto them, "abstain from consuming human sacrifices, but immolate no creature to whom life has been given, for all things that exist have been created for the profit of man.

15 "Do not steal the goods of your neighbor, for that would be to deprive him of what he has acquired by the sweat of his brow.

16 "Deceive no one, so as not to be yourselves deceived. Endeavor to justify yourself before the last judgment, for then it will be too late.

17 "Do not give yourselves up to debauchery, for that would be to violate the laws of God.

18 "You shall attain to supreme happiness, not only in purifying yourselves, but also in guiding others in the way that shall permit them to gain original perfection."

CHAPTER VIII

1 The neighboring countries resounded with the prophecies of Issa, and when he entered into Persia the priests became alarmed and forbade the inhabitants to listen to him.

2 And when they saw all the villages welcoming him with joy and listening devoutly to his sermons, they gave orders to arrest him and had him brought before the high priest, where he underwent the following interrogation:

3 "Of what new God cost thou speak? Art thou not aware, unhappy man, that Saint Zoroaster is the only just one admitted to the privilege of communion with the Supreme Being,

4 "Who ordered the angels to put down in writing the word of God for the use of his people, laws that were given to Zoroaster in paradise?

5 "Who then art thou to dare here to blaspheme our God and to sow doubt in the hearts of believers?"

6 And Issa said unto them: "It is not of a new God that I speak but of our Heavenly Father, who has existed since all time and who will still be after the end of all things.

7 "It is of him that I have discoursed to the people, who, like unto innocent children, are not yet capable of comprehending God by the simple strength of their intelligence or of penetrating into his divine and spiritual sublimity.

8 "But even as a babe discovers in the darkness its mother's breast, so even your people, who have been led into error by your erroneous doctrine and your religious ceremonies, have recognized by instinct their Father in the Father of whom I am the prophet.

9 "The Eternal Being has said to your people through the medium of my mouth: 'You shall not worship the sun, for it is but a part of the world which I have created for man.

10 "'The sun rises in order to warm you during your work; it sets to allow you the repose which I myself have appointed.

11 "'It is to me, and to me alone, that you owe all that you possess, all that is to be found about you, above you, and below you.'"

12 "But," said the priests, "how could a people live according to the rules of justice if it had no preceptors?"

13 Then Issa answered, "So long as the people had no priests, the natural law governed them, and they preserved the candor of their souls.

14 "Their souls were with God, and to commune with the Father they had recourse to the medium of no idol or animal, nor to the fire, as is practiced here.

15 "You contend that one must worship the sun, the spirit of good and of evil. Well, I say unto you, your doctrine is a false one, the sun acting not spontaneously but according to the will of the invisible Creator who gave it birth

16 "And who has willed it to be the star that should light the day, to warm the labor and the seedtime of man.

17 "The Eternal Spirit is the soul of all that is animate. You commit a great sin in dividing it into a spirit of evil and a spirit of good, for there is no God outside the good,

18 "Who, like unto the father of a family, does but good to his children, forgiving all their faults if they repent them.

19 "The spirit of evil dwells on the earth in the hearts of those men who turn aside the children of God from the strait path.

20 "Wherefore I say unto you, Beware of the day of judgment, for God will inflict a terrible chastisement upon all those who shall have led his children astray from the right path and have filled them with superstitions and prejudices;

21 "Those who have blinded them that see, conveyed contagion to the healthy, and taught the worship of the things that God has subordinated to man for his good and to aid him in his work.

22 "Your doctrine is therefore the fruit of your errors; for desiring to bring near to you the God of truth, you have created for yourselves false gods."

23 After having listened to him, the magi determined to do him no harm. But at night, when all the town lay sleeping, they conducted him outside of the walls and abandoned him on the high road, in the hope that he would soon become a prey to the wild beasts.

24 But, protected by the Lord our God, Saint Issa continued his way unmolested.

CHAPTER IX

1 Issa, whom the Creator had elected to remind a depraved humanity of the true God, had reached his twenty-ninth year when he returned to the land of Israel.

2 Since his departure the pagans had inflicted still more atrocious sufferings on the Israelites, who were a prey to the deepest despondency.

3 Many among them had already begun to abandon the laws of their God and those of Mossa in the hope of appeasing their savage conquerors.

4 In the face of this evil, Issa exhorted his compatriots not to despair because the day of the redemption of sins was at hand, and he confirmed them in the belief which they had in the God of their fathers.

5 "Children, do not give yourselves up to despair," said the Heavenly Father by the mouth of Issa, "for I have heard your voice, and your cries have reached me.

6 "Do not weep, O my beloved ones! For your grief has touched the heart of your Father, and he has forgiven you, even as he forgave your forefathers.

7 "Do not abandon your families to plunge yourselves into debauchery, do not lose the nobility of your feelings, and do not worship idols who will remain deaf to your voices.

8 "Fill my temple with your hope and with your patience and abjure not the religion of your fathers; for I alone have guided them and have heaped them with benefits.

9 "You shall lift up those who have fallen, you shall give food to the hungry, and you shall come to the aid of the sick, so as to be all pure and just at the day of the last judgment which I prepare for you."

10 The Israelites came in crowds at the word of Issa, asking him where they should praise the Heavenly Father, seeing that the enemy had razed their temples to the ground and laid low their sacred vessels.

11 And Issa made answer to them that God had not in view temples erected by the hands of man, but he meant that the human heart was the true temple of God.

12 "Enter into your temple, into your heart. Illumine it with good thoughts and the patience and immovable confidence which you should have in your Father.

13 "And your sacred vessels, they are your hands and your eyes. See and do that which is agreeable to God, for in doing good to your neighbor you accomplish a rite which embellishes the temple wherein dwells he who gave you life.

14 "For God has created you in his own likeness-innocent, with pure souls and hearts filled with goodness, destined not for the conception of evil schemes but made to be sanctuaries of love and justice.

15 "Wherefore I say unto you, sully not your hearts, for the Supreme Being dwells therein eternally.

16 "If you wish to accomplish works marked with love or piety, do them with an open heart and let not your actions be governed by calculations or the hope of gain.

17 "For such actions would not help to your salvation, and you would fall into that state of moral degradation where theft, lying, and murder pass for generous deeds."

CHAPTER X

1 Saint Issa went from one town to another, strengthening by the word of God the courage of the Israelites, who were ready to succumb to the weight of their despair; and thousands of men followed him to hear him preach.

2 But the chiefs of the towns became afraid of him, and they made known to the principal governor who dwelt at Jerusalem that a man named Issa had arrived in the country; that he was stirring up by his discourses the people against the authorities; that the crowd listened to him with assiduity, neglected the works of the state, and affirmed that before long it would be rid of its intrusive governors.

3 Then Pilate, governor of Jerusalem, ordered that they should seize the person of the preacher Issa, that they

should bring him into the town and lead him before the judges. But in order not to excite the anger of the populace, Pilate charged the priests and the learned Hebrew elders to judge him in the temple.

4 Meanwhile Issa, continuing his preachings, arrived at Jerusalem; and, having learnt of his arrival, all the inhabitants, knowing him already by reputation, went out to meet him.

5 They greeted him respectfully and opened to him the gates of their temple in order to hear from his mouth what he had said in the other cities of Israel.

6 And Issa said unto them: "The human race perishes because of its lack of faith, for the darkness and the tempest have scattered the flocks of humanity and they have lost their shepherds.

7 "But the tempest will not last forever, and the darkness will not always obscure the light. The sky will become once more serene, the heavenly light will spread itself over the earth, and the flocks gone astray will gather around their shepherd.

8 "Do not strive to find straight paths in the darkness, lest ye fall into a pit; but gather together your remaining strength, support one another, place your confidence in your God, and wait till light appears.

9 "He who sustains his neighbor, sustains himself; and whosoever protects his family, protects the people and the state.

10 "For be sure that the day is at hand when you shall be delivered from the darkness; you shall be gathered together as one family; and your enemy, who ignores what the favor of God is, shall tremble with fear."

11 The priests and the elders who were listening to him, filled with admiration at his discourse, asked him if it were true that he had tried to stir up the people against the authorities of the country, as had been reported to the governor Pilate.

12 "Can one excite to insurrection men gone astray, from whom the obscurity has hidden their door and their path?" replied Issa. "I have only warned the unfortunate, as I do here in this temple, that they may not further advance along the darkened way, for an abyss is open under their feet.

13 "Earthly power is not of long duration, and it is subject to many changes. Of what use that man should revolt against it, seeing that one power always succeeds to another power? And thus it will come to pass until the extinction of humanity.

14 "Against which, see you not that the mighty and the rich sow among the sons of Israel a spirit of rebellion against the eternal power of heaven?"

15 The elders then asked: "Who art thou, and from what country cost thou come? We have not heard speak of thee before, and we know not even thy name."

16 "I am an Israelite," replied Issa. "From the day of my birth I saw the walls of Jerusalem, and I heard the weeping of my brothers reduced to slavery and the lamentations of my sisters who were carried away by the pagans.

17 "And my soul was filled with sadness when I saw that my brethren had forgotten the true God. As a child, I left my father's house and went to dwell among other peoples.

18 "But having heard that my brethren were suffering still greater tortures, I have come back to the country where my parents dwell to remind my brothers of the faith of their forefathers, which teaches us patience on earth to obtain perfect and sublime happiness in heaven."

19 And the learned elders put him this question: "It is said that thou deniest the laws of Mossa and that thou teaches" the people to forsake the temple of God?"

20 And Issa replied: "One cannot demolish that which has been given by our Heavenly Father, neither that which has been destroyed by sinners; but I have enjoined the

purification of the heart from all blemish, for it is the true temple of God.

21 "As to the laws of Mossa, I have endeavored to establish them in the hearts of men. And I say unto you that you do not understand their real meaning, for it is not vengeance but mercy that they teach; only the sense of these laws has been perverted."

CHAPTER XI

1 Having hearkened unto Issa, the priests and the wise elders decided among themselves not to judge him, for he did harm to no one. And presenting themselves before Pilate, appointed governor of Jerusalem by the pagan king of the country of Romeles, they addressed him thus:

2 "We have seen the man whom thou accusest of inciting our people to rebellion; we have heard his discourses, and we know him to be our compatriot.

3 "But the chiefs of the cities have made thee false reports, for this is a just man who teaches the people the word of God. After having interrogated him, we dismissed him, that he might go in peace."

4 The governor then became enraged and sent near to Issa his servants in disguise, so that they might watch all his actions and report to the authorities the least word that he should address to the people.

5 In the meantime, Saint Issa continued to visit the neighboring towns, preaching the true ways of the Creator, exhorting the Hebrews to patience, and promising them a speedy deliverance.

6 And during all this time, many people followed him wherever he went, several never leaving him but becoming his servitors.

7 And Issa said: "Do not believe in miracles wrought by the hand of man, for he who dominates over nature is alone capable of doing that which is supernatural, whilst man is

powerless to stay the anger of the winds or to spread the rain.

8 "Nevertheless, there is one miracle which it is possible for man to accomplish. It is when, full of a sincere belief, he decides to root out from his heart all evil thoughts, and when to attain his end he forsakes the paths of iniquity.

9 "And all the things that are done without God are but errors, seductions, and enchantments, which only demonstrate to what an extent the soul of him who practices this art is full of shamelessness, falsehood, and impurity.

10 "Put not your faith in oracles; God alone knows the future: he who has recourse to diviners profanes the temple which is in his heart and gives a proof of distrust towards his Creator.

11 "Faith in diviners and in their oracles destroys the innate simplicity of man and his childlike purity. An infernal power takes possession of him, forcing him to commit all sorts of crimes and to worship idols;

12 "Whereas the Lord our God, who has no equal, is one, all-mighty, omniscient, and omnipresent. It is he who possesses all wisdom and all light.

13 "It is to him you must address yourselves to be consoled in your sorrows, helped in your works, and cured in your sickness. Whosoever shall have recourse to him shall not be denied.

14 "The secret of nature is in the hands of God. For the world, before it appeared, existed in the depth of the divine thought; it became material and visible by the will of the Most High.

15 "When you address yourselves to him, become again as children; for you know neither the past, the present, nor the future, and God is the Master of all time."

CHAPTER XII

1 "Righteous man," said unto him the spies of the governor of Jerusalem, "tell us if we shall perform the will of our Caesar or await our speedy deliverance."

2 And Issa, having recognized them as people appointed to follow him, replied: "I have not said to you that you shall be delivered from Caesar. It is the soul plunged in error that shall have its deliverance.

3 "As there can be no family without a head, so there can be no order among a people without a Caesar; to him implicit obedience should be given, he alone being answerable for his acts before the supreme tribunal."

4 "Does Caesar possess a divine right?" further asked of him the spies. "And is he the best of mortals?"

5 "There should be no better among men, but there are also sufferers, whom those elected and charged with this mission should care for, making use of the means conferred on them by the sacred law of our Heavenly Father.

6 "Mercy and justice are the highest attributes of a Caesar; his name will be illustrious if he adhere to them.

7 "But he who acts otherwise, who exceeds the limit of power that he has over his subordinates, going so far as to put their lives in danger, offends the great Judge and loses his dignity in the sight of man."

8 At this juncture, an old woman who had approached the group, the better to hear Issa, was pushed aside by one of the spies, who placed himself before her.

9 Then Issa held forth: "It is not meet that a son should set aside his mother, taking her place. Whosoever respecteth not his mother, the most sacred being after his God, is unworthy of the name of son.

10 "Listen, then, to what I say unto you: Respect woman, for she is the mother of the universe, and all the truth of divine creation lies in her.

11 "She is the basis of all that is good and beautiful, as she is also the germ of life and death. On her depends the

whole existence of man, for she is his natural and moral support.

12 "She gives birth to you in the midst of suffering. By the sweat of her brow she rears you, and until her death you cause her the gravest anxieties. Bless her and worship her, for she is your one friend, your one support on earth.

13 "Respect her, uphold her. In acting thus you will win her love and her heart. You will find favor in the sight of God and many sins shall be forgiven you.

14 "In the same way, love your wives and respect them; for they will be mothers tomorrow, and each later on the ancestress of a race.

15 "Be lenient towards woman. Her love ennobles man, softens his hardened heart, tames the brute in him, and makes of him a lamb.

16 "The wife and the mother are the inappreciable treasures given unto you by God. They are the fairest ornaments of existence, and of them shall be born all the inhabitants of the world.

17 "Even as the God of armies separated of old the light from the darkness and the land from the waters, woman possesses the divine faculty of separating in a man good intentions from evil thoughts.

18 "Wherefore I say unto you, after God your best thoughts should belong to the women and the wives, woman being for you the temple wherein you will obtain the most easily perfect happiness.

19 "Imbue yourselves in this temple with moral strength. Here you will forget your sorrows and your failures, and you will recover the lost energy necessary to enable you to help your neighbor.

20 "Do not expose her to humiliation. In acting thus you would humiliate yourselves and lose the sentiment of love, without which nothing exists here below.

21 "Protect your wife, in order that she may protect you and all your family. All that you do for your wife, your

mother, for a widow or another woman in distress, you will have done unto your God."

CHAPTER XIII
1 Saint Issa taught the people of Israel thus for three years, in every town, in every village, by the waysides and on the plains; and all that he had predicted came to pass.
2 During all this time the disguised servants of Pilate watched him closely without hearing anything said like unto the reports made against Issa in former years by the chiefs of the towns.
3 But the governor Pilate, becoming alarmed at the too great popularity of Saint Issa, who according to his adversaries sought to stir up the people to proclaim him king, ordered one of his spies to accuse him.
4 Then soldiers were commanded to proceed to his arrest, and they imprisoned him in a subterranean cell where they tortured him in various ways in the hope of forcing him to make a confession which should permit of his being put to death.
5 The saint, thinking only of the perfect beatitude of his brethren, supported all his sufferings in the name of his Creator.
6 The servants of Pilate continued to torture him and reduced him to a state of extreme weakness; but God was with him and did not allow him to die.
7 Learning of the sufferings and the tortures which their saint was enduring, the high priests and the wise elders went to pray the governor to set Issa at liberty in honor of an approaching festival.
8 But the governor straightway refused them this. They then prayed him to allow Issa to appear before the tribunal of the ancients so that he might be condemned or acquitted before the festival, and to this Pilate consented.

9 The next day the governor assembled together the chief captains, priests, wise elders, and lawyers so that they might judge Issa.

10 They brought him from his prison and seated him before the governor between two thieves to be judged at the same time as he, in order to show unto the crowd that he was not the only one to be condemned.

11 And Pilate, addressing himself to Issa, said unto him: "O man! is it true that thou incites" the people against the authorities with the intent of thyself becoming king of Israel?"

12 "One becomes not king at one's own will," replied Issa, "and they have lied who have told thee that I stir up the people to rebellion. I have never spoken of other than the King of Heaven, and it is he I teach the people to worship.

13 "For the sons of Israel have lost their original purity; and if they have not recourse to the true God, they will be sacrificed and their temple shall fall into ruins.

14 "As temporal power maintains order in a country, I teach them accordingly not to forget it. I say unto them: 'Live conformably to your station and your fortune, so as not to disturb the public order.' And I have exhorted them also to remember that disorder reigns in their hearts and in their minds.

15 "Wherefore the King of Heaven has punished them and suppressed their national kings. Nevertheless, I have said unto them, 'If you become resigned to your destinies, as a reward the kingdom of heaven shall be reserved for you.'"

16 At this moment, the witnesses were brought forward, one of whom made the following deposition: "Thou hast said to the people that the temporal power is as naught against that of the king who shall soon deliver the Israelites from the pagan yoke."

17 "Blessed art thou," said Issa, "for having spoken the truth. The King of Heaven is greater and more powerful

A Broader View

than the terrestrial law, and his kingdom surpasses all the kingdoms of the earth.

18 "And the time is not far off when, conforming to the divine will, the people of Israel shall purify them of their sins; for it has been said that a forerunner will come to proclaim the deliverance of the people, gathering them into one fold."

19 And the governor, addressing himself to the judges, said: "Doss hear? The Israelite Issa confesses to the crime of which he is accused. Judge him, then, according to your laws, and pronounce against him capital punishment."

20 "We cannot condemn him," replied the priests and the elders. "Thou hast just heard thyself that his allusions were made regarding the King of Heaven and that he has preached naught to the sons of Israel which could constitute an offense against the law."

21 The governor Pilate then sent for the witness who, at his instigation, had betrayed Issa. The man came and addressed Issa thus: "Didst thou not pass thyself off as the king of Israel when thou saddest that he who reigns in the heavens had sent thee to prepare his people?"

22 And Issa, having blessed him, said: "Thou shalt be pardoned, for what thou sayest does not come from thee!" Then, addressing himself to the governor: "Why humiliate thy dignity, and why teach thy inferiors to live in falsehood, as without doing so thou hast power to condemn the innocent?"

23 At these words the governor became exceeding wroth, ordering the sentence of death to be passed upon Issa and the acquittal of the two thieves.

24 The judges, having consulted together, said unto Pilate: "We will not take upon our heads the great sin of condemning an innocent man and acquitting thieves. That would be against the law.

25 "Do then as thou wilt." Saying which the priests and the wise elders went out and washed their hands in a sacred

A BROADER VIEW

vessel, saying: "We are innocent of the death of this just man."

CHAPTER XIV

1 By the order of the governor, the soldiers then seized Issa and the two thieves, whom they led to the place of execution, where they nailed them to crosses erected on the ground.
2 All the day the bodies of Issa and the two thieves remained suspended, terrible to behold, under the guard of the soldiers; the people standing all around, the relations of the sufferers praying and weeping.
3 At sunset the sufferings of Issa came to an end. He lost consciousness, and the soul of this just man left his body to become absorbed in the Divinity.
4 Thus ended the earthly existence of the reflection of the Eternal Spirit under the form of a man who had saved hardened sinners and endured many sufferings.
5 Meanwhile, Pilate became afraid of his action and gave the body of the saint to his parents, who buried it near the spot of hisexecution. The crowd came to pray over his tomb, and the air was filled with groans and lamentations.
6 Three days after, the governor sent his soldiers to carry away the body of Issa to bury it elsewhere, fearing otherwise a popular insurrection.
7 The next day the crowd found the tomb open and empty. At once the rumor spread that the supreme Judge had sent his angels to carry away the mortal remains of the saint in whom dwelt on earth a part of the Divine Spirit.
8 When this rumor reached the knowledge of Pilate, he became angered and forbade anyone, under the pain of slavery and death, to pronounce the name of Issa or to pray the Lord for him.
9 But the people continued to weep and to glorify aloud their Master; wherefore many were led into captivity, subjected to torture, and put to death.

10 And the disciples of Saint Issa abandoned the land of Israel and scattered themselves among the heathen, preaching that they should renounce their errors, bethink them of the salvation of their souls and of the perfect felicity awaiting humanity in that immaterial world of light where, in repose and in all his purity, the Great Creator dwells in perfect majesty.

11 The pagans, their kings, and their warriors listened to the preachers, abandoned their absurd beliefs, and forsook their priests and their idols to celebrate the praise of the all-wise Creator of the universe, the King of kings, whose heart is filled with infinite mercy.

A Broader View

Chapter Seven
About Islam

In a study of Christ and Christianity, it is important to understand something about Islam and its history. The two religions have crossed paths many times. Judaism, Christianity, and Islam are the faiths of the Children of Abraham. And though it seems unlikely given today's circumstances, at some point in time these three faiths must find some harmony, some sense of mutual appreciation and cooperation.

Islam means "submission," as in submission to Allah, to God. *Muslim* or *Moslem* means "those who submit." The story of Islam begins with its prophet.

Mohammed or Muhammad was born in the city of Mecca (*Makkah* in Arabic) in Arabia in 570 AD He came from a respected and prominent family. When he was 25 he married a wealthy widow named Khadija. Their marriage was happy. Their only child to live to maturity was a daughter named Fatima. Mohammed spent much of his time in solitary meditation. Originally he followed the polytheistic gods of the Arabs, numbering over 250. Around 610 AD, Mohammed had a religious experience that changed his life. It began with the hearing of a divine voice that he later believed to be the angel Gabriel. This is the same Gabriel of the Jewish and Christian religions – the angelic deliverer of the prophecy to Daniel and the announcer to Mary of her special pregnancy.

Gabriel directed Mohammed to: "Recite, in the name of the Lord who has created, created man from clots of blood; Recite, seeing that the Lord is the most generous, who has taught by the pen, taught man what he did not know." The Arabic word for "recite" is *Qur'an* (Koran), meaning the reciting or the reading. Therefore, the sacred book of the Muslims, Qur'an, is the "recitings" of revelations given to Mohammed. Over a period of 22 years, Mohammed recorded his revelations. The Koran contains 114 chapters of Mohammed's divinely inspired revelations.

According to Mohammed, Judaism and Christianity greatly influenced his religious understanding. He considered himself to be of the descendants of Abraham, from the line of Abraham's son Ishmael.

In one of his visions, Gabriel tells Mohammed that Allah [literally "the God" in Arabic] is the only god and that he is to adopt the name of "Prophet." He is directed to go out and convert the "Quaraish," a tribe in Saudi Arabia, to accept that there is only one God and Mohammed is his prophet. Encouraged by his wife, he began to preach in the streets and market places of Mecca.

His preaching was met with bitter opposition, but for many years his influential uncle, Abu Talib, was able to protect him. When both his wife Khadija and his uncle Abu Talib died in 620, plots were hatched to kill Mohammed and his followers. On July 16, 622, Mohammed was forced to flee Mecca and go to Medina, a friendlier city to the north. This flight, called the *hegira*, marks the beginning of Islam. The Muslim calendar starts with this date, and the years are counted from "A.H." meaning "after hegira."

In Medina, Mohammed's message was well received. He eventually became the religious and political leader of Medina.

Soon the Meccans organized an army to destroy Mohammed and his followers in Medina. In 630, Mohammed and his armies defeated the challengers, and triumphant, they entered Mecca and destroyed every idol in the Kabah (*Kaaba* in Arabic, meaning "cube"), which was the main temple, except the "Black Stone," a sacred meteorite enshrined there. Mohammed then declared the Kabah to be the most holy shrine in Islam. Since that time it has been the spot to which all devout Muslims direct their prayers.

The legend is that the Kabah is in the shape of the "House in Heaven" called *Baitul Ma'amoor*. God directed that such a shrine be built on a corresponding place on the Earth and Adam was the first to build this shrine. The first "House of Heaven" on Earth was built at Mecca by Adam under God's direction, thus making it a Holy Place. Later, Abraham and his son Ishmael built it again or rebuilt it. In the Koran, sura 2, verse127, it says: "As Abraham (*Ibrahim* in Arabic) raised the foundations of the shrine, together with Ishmael, they prayed: 'Our Lord, accept this from us. You are the Hearer, the Omniscient.'"

For the next two years, Mohammed strengthened his position as the prophet and ruler of Arabia. He united the tribes into a vast army to conquer the world for Allah. His death in 632 AD did not lessen the fervor of his followers.

In today's news we hear little of the spirituality of Islam. The news is all about Islam's strict laws, holy-war mentality, and intolerance for nonbelievers. The militant extremists get all of the headlines. Islam has become known as the religion of fanatical terrorists. The greater truth is that Islam has produced many marvelous centuries of science, mathematics, literature, architecture, and high culture, even mystical movements throughout its roughly 1,400 years of existence. In the 1960s and 70s in North America and Europe, there was widespread interest in Sufism, classical Sufism. Amazingly, many Westerners who studied and practice this mystical way had no idea that it was Islamic in origin.

Sufis were Muslims who professed a belief in and a devotion to the union of one's soul directly with God – a classic definition for any religion's mysticism. One might say that this movement began with the Prophet himself, Mohammed, who entered into altered states of consciousness to hear the voice of Gabriel conveying God's message. But the first stage of Sufism appeared in asceticism among pious circles as a reaction against worldliness, from about 661 to 749 AD From their practice of constantly meditating on the Koranic words about Doomsday, the ascetics became known as "those who always weep" and those who consider this world "a hut of sorrows." They were also distinguished by their partiality for nighttime prayers. Sufism became a separate school of thought and practice around 922 AD, when a Baghdad mystic, al-Hallaj cried out from his ecstatic union with God, "I am the Truth!" For which he was quickly executed for blasphemy. This was an experience which Jesus could certainly appreciate.

After al-Hallaj's execution, the Sufis, or mystics, whose views had been increasingly in conflict with the mainline Islamic teachers of religious law, moved westward to Persia (modern-day Iran) where they were tolerated. By the 1100s Sufi missionaries carried mystical Islamic preaching and practices to the urban working class and the countryside.

From 1132 to 1212, Islam was at a high point, its religion, science, art, poetry, and culture stretched from Spain to India and all of North Africa, including Egypt. But it all began to turn around in 1220 with the Mongol invasions of Genghis Khan into India, Pakistan, Afghanistan, Iran, and Iraq. Amazingly, the Mongols could not maintain their hold on the people because they themselves began to enjoyed the rich Islamic culture, and rapidly became assimilated into it, causing their wide barbaric spirit to clam. Eventually, future Khans (most notably, Il-Khan) allowed their soldiers to be Buddhists, Christians, or non-Sunni Muslims. However, Ghazan Khan later embraced Islam amid general acceptance by his army, and all his successors where Muslims.

The Mongol invasions were followed by the Mamluk invasions, military slaves who gained power in Egypt. These were followed by the Ottoman Turks. Both the Mamluks and the Ottomans were Muslim, and since the Mongols converted to Islam, the region never lost full contact with its principle faith. However, it did suffer a series of destructions and unstable governments.

It is interesting to note that the greatest Mamluk general and sultan was Saladin, who was victorious over King Richard the Lionheart in the Crusades. Osama bin Laden, the modern Islamic terrorist, claims to be Saladin's spirit returned.

These military invasions took their toll on the cultural achievements of Islam. Islam has always had a close connection with military power. Many of its nations were run by military leaders, many continue to be so today. In the midst of the destruction of governments and institutions caused by these invasions and uprisings, the mystical Sufis continued to experience God and express their experiences in art and literature, but most of this was now confined to Turkey and Persia (Iran). The great mystical poet and teacher Jalal ad-Din ar-Rumi and his son Sultan Walad both wrote and published in Turkey, helping to fill the artistic vacuum left by military control.

The cultural declines in the 1200s were turned around a century later, when Islam experienced a renaissance of its culture from Spain and Northern Africa to India. During this time Islam expanded into the Malay islands, Africa south of the Sahara, and into southern Russia. Amazingly, the function of maintaining unity among all these diverse groups was given to the mystics, the Sufi orders or "paths," as they were called; mainly because they had endured so well in the prior centuries. But fundamentalism was coming, and it would not tolerate mystical insights and genteel poetry and art. The words and laws of the Koran were all anyone needed or should need.

Fundamentalism's rise to power came in some respects as a reaction to mystics who had become too antirational and subjective, without connecting or correlating the original words from God through Gabriel into daily life. A fundamentalist backlash, begun in the 800s by Ahmad ibn Hanbal and carried on by Ibn Taymiyah in the early 1300s, went far beyond rebalancing Koranic law with mystical experiences. The Islamic rulers began to war among themselves. A kind of predatory mentality grew among those in power and fratricidal wars began (killing of one's brothers and sisters).

Through much of this conflict, the personal-relationship-with-God message of the Sufis endured. The missionary spirit in Sufism operated amazingly well in times of political instability. In India, the Sufi message of mysticism, asceticism, and universalism struck a deep chord in the Indian temperament. Sufi teachers contrasted so much with the aloofness, elitism, and contempt for all things Hindu by the first wave of Muslim invaders, that Indians of the lower castes found Sufi Islam warm and thoughtful, and converted to it readily. But this Islam was not the Islam of the orthodox Muslims, who believed Indian Muslims could eroded the purity of Islam and moved to stop the Sufis. The fundamentalists gained power and demanded that the Mughal emperor execute his brother, a princely Sufi mystic named Dara Shikoh for heresy in 1659.

In the 1700s, in Iraq and Iran, Mohammed Baqir Bihbihani attacked Sufism, shutting their school and insisting that the religious scholars (*mujtahids*) are the real leaders of Shi'ite Islam. In 1762 in India, a Sufi leader and his students began a movement back to the law, discarding both traditionalism and mystical experience. By the 1800s, with Western imperialism reaching every corner of the Earth, a movement away from universalism to a strict focus on Muslims as one people, one nation, one civilization, intrinsically superior to the decadent West grew, and in many areas continues today. World War I and II brought alien forces upon the Muslim world that they could neither evade nor control. This was followed by the colonization of Palestine by Zionists (Jews who believe that Palestine is their rightful and natural homeland) in the late 1940s and 50s. The state of Israel was established with Western financial, diplomatic, and military support. Islam found itself growing increasingly dependent upon Soviet assistance against Western imperialistic forces. For Muslims, the ultimate dramatization of this was the attack by the United Kingdom, Israel, and France upon Egypt following the nationalization in 1956 of the Suez Canal, with American money behind it all. Eventually, Western imperialism stopped, with the West retreating from their former colonies.

Today, virtually all Muslims have obtained independence from foreign domination (except in Russia and Chinese Central Asia). Sufism is now a shadow of its former self and a very small part of modern Islam. Most all Muslims are orthodox, and many are fundamentalists. Even among modern Sufi organizations, the members are no longer mystics, holding closer to the law and words of God rather than to personal experiences of God's presence and guidance. As indicated before, in the 1960s and '70s, Sufism found fertile fields in the youth of the Western World (Europe, England, and the United States).

Sufism revered music as an aid to ecstatic states of consciousness with God. The tambourine and pipe were played using repetitive rhythms with chanting and dancing. The famous Whirling Dervishes of Turkey were Sufis seeking to experience direct sense of God's presence. The rhythms and movement helped the participants to forget the things around them, leading them to experience *fana*, meaning "extinction," in which they lost awareness of their sense of a physical self. The idea behind this is expressed in a quote from the Koran, sura 55, verses 26-27: "All in the created world will pass away, but the face of your Lord will remain."

Rabi 'a al-Adawiyya (late 700s), a woman Sufi (of which there were many) is credited with creating Islamic mysticism from asceticism by adding *love*. Love for God turned the lean discipline of the ascetics into the Sufis' warm caring for others, both for their needs and their education, and their missionary spirit. She wrote the following: "O God, if I worship You for fear of hell, burn me in hell; If I worship You in hope of paradise, exclude me from paradise; But if I worship You for Your own sake, Grudge me not Your everlasting beauty."

The Nubian Sufi, Dhu an-Nun (early 800s) introduced the concept of "interior knowledge" (*ma'rifah*) as opposed to learned knowledge. This gave each person a sense of their direct contact with Truth and potential guidance from within.

Poetry, hymns, art, and music all expressed the Sufis' love for God and joy in sharing this with others, even foreigners. There are reports of Sufis meeting Christian hermits, and sharing their mutual love for God.

The many plumed Simurgh bird is a symbol of Sufi desires for unity with the Divine. A Persian poem tells of how other birds who had seen the Simurgh's splendor set off to find him. Only 30 birds survived the search, and when they reached his mountain they realized that he and they were really one! The Simurgh bird was composed of all the birds. In Persian, *si murgh* means "30 birds." It is reminiscent of the *E Pluribus Unum* on U.S. coins: "out of many, one."

Sufis often taught by telling stories that had deep insights into truths that were otherwise difficult to grasp.

A Broader View

An example is the wonderful Sufi tale about blind men describing an elephant each from their own particular contact with the creature: one says it's like a rope since he's holding the tail, another says it's like a hose since he's holding the trunk, another says it's like a broad wall since he's touching the side, another says it's tall and skinny since he's touching the leg – all being right of course, from their individual contact points.

Another insightful Sufi story is a lesson in how distractions during meditation may be avoided. The story goes like this: A holy man was sitting by the side of the road meditating, when a woman on her way to the marketplace to shop for her family walked by. The woman's skirt touched the holy man, causing him to come out of his meditation and yell at her, "Woman, I was with God when your skirt struck me!" To which the woman replied, "Oh, I'm so sorry. I was so focused on my family's needs that I didn't notice you." At this point in the story the Sufi teacher stops and asks the listeners which of these two was in the deeper meditation?

Of course, chief among mystics in all religions is the belief in divine revelation that is personally received during contact with God, or God's angels or forces. In Sufism, this was called *kashf*. Intuition was distinct from revelation, and was called *wahy*. As with all mystical movements, the concept of revelation poses a threat to theologians. For them, revelation is too subjective. It is wiser and more objective to be led by the holy scriptures and their laws. Even in Islam many teach that the mystical experiences of Mohammed, receiving the original knowledge during an ecstatic state, brought the law to mankind for them to live by, not encouraging mankind to experience the states of consciousness with the Divine that Mohammed did. Sufism attempted to resolve this conflict with the concept of a rhythmic movement between the inner and outer life, between the oneness and the multiplicity. With this concept in mind, the inner experience was honored and the outer activity was set according to the law and scriptures. The ultimate state in Far Eastern mysticism is *nirvana*, in Sufi mysticism it is *haquqah*, "reality." This state is often referred to as the "second sobriety," indicating the return of the completely transformed mystic into this world to act as a witness of God and to continue the physical journey *with* God. Islam today is in a very different faith than what was just described. But within it there is a struggle to rediscover the faith's deepest beliefs and spirit. Now that Islamic terrorists are killing Muslims, there is a heightened sense of desperation to get a hold on this militant energy. Islamic extremists have now taken the struggle to their own people, their own faith. It remains to be seen how this will all end.

Made in the USA
Columbia, SC
16 March 2019